French Country Cooking

Authentic Recipes from Every Region

FRANÇOISE BRANGET

TRANSLATED FROM THE FRENCH BY
JEANNETTE SEAVER

ARCADE PUBLISHING · NEW YORK

Arcade Publishing books may be purchased in bulk at special discounts for sales promotion, corporate gifts, fund-raising, or educational purposes. Special editions can also be created to specifications. For details, contact the Special Sales Department, Arcade Publishing, 307 West 36th Street, 11th Floor, New York, NY 10018 or arcade@skyhorsepublishing.com.

Arcade Publishing® is a registered trademark of Skyhorse Publishing, Inc.®, a Delaware corporation.

Visit our website at www.arcadepub.com.

10 9 8 7 6 5 4 3 2 1

Library of Congress Cataloging-in-Publication Data is available on file.

Cover design by Laura Klynstra

Print ISBN: 978-1-62872-590-2
Ebook ISBN: 978-1-61145-858-9

Printed in China

Contents

Amuse Bouche:
A Little Taste of What Is to Follow

Politics and cuisine?

While this might seem an unlikely combination at first glance, the two share singular affinities.

Ambassadors of their departments, French deputies represent their constituents at the Palais Bourbon, home of the National Assembly—the forum where France conducts its politics. Beyond the political aspect of their role, however, these deputies all enjoy good cuisine, and have agreed to share and exhibit with pride a sample of the gastronomy of their particular land—*le terroir*. Each recipe, each dish is made with the prized products, meat and sea fare, identified with their district.

This book is the personal mirror of various culinary traditions born in the course of a long history, passed down through the generations. Today each traditional cuisine, while retaining its authenticity, has traveled beyond its original borders and can be enjoyed throughout all of France—and the world.

Like the scope of their politics, the various regional cuisines presented in this book can be modest or grand, innovative or orthodox, stimulating or soothing. The one basic common denominator is the quality of the products and ingredients assembled for each preparation. Combining flavors is the second act that will determine whether a magical dish appears on the table.

Every five years, deputies in France stand for election, in a sort of grand electoral cook-off. Candidates may get roasted, skewered, raked over the coals, stewed in their own juices, or grilled by their constituents, but at the end of day all are in the same position, presented on the same platter. Both crusty veterans and young sprouts are subject to the electorate's scrutiny, and only the candidates best able to respond to the issues of the moment will get the thumbs-up and avoid the compost heap.

In *French Country Cooking: Authentic Recipes from Every Region*, for the first time, deputies representing every department of metropolitan France, including our overseas territories, have contributed to a collective cookbook offering savory and sweet, time-tested and timeless dishes.

It is with great pleasure that I invite you to share the panoply of gourmand moments with us. You will discover never-published recipes, and will even be surprised by some new combinations of flavors.

My hope is that reading this book will inspire your own creativity, as well as ignite your curiosity to explore our rich and multifaceted country.

Françoise Branget
Deputy of Doubs

Notes from the American Editor and Translator

This book, an armchair travelogue of France with recipes emblematic of each district, will give the reader a rare opportunity of discovering *la France profonde*, off the beaten track.

Endowed with landscapes as rich as they are diverse, fertile farmlands and orchards throughout, France's singular patrimony is its incredibly varied gastronomy—an art refined over centuries.

History points out that a great many of the dishes considered today part of our gastronomic glory trace their roots to a time when rural France suffered extreme poverty. The only way for the countrymen to survive was to avail themselves of all the simple elements growing nearby. Some plants they gathered from nature's bounty, and some they grew themselves. Every possible part was used, either to feed the family, to fertilize the fields, or to feed the livestock. And the animals—besides producing milk or eggs or offspring—were in turn used for food from head to hoof. Driven by necessity, the rural householder learned how best to utilize each part of the beef or lamb, pig or chicken, including delicacies made of the innards and the extremities.

The recipes in this book for the most part date from long ago, emanating from the rural *terroir*, the small villages of *la France profonde*, from a time when farmers' choices to feed themselves were limited to the produce of their own land—and when native creativity and innate ingenuity arose to transform the most humble ingredients into delectable fare.

Most of the deputies in the French Parliament who contributed to this collection were handed down a recipe by a grandmother or mother, secrets of family lore. Their sharing of their closely guarded treasures enables today's reader to enjoy traditional cooking and to survey the origins of French gastronomy.

From these timeworn memoranda, scribbled in patois or local dialect and for the most part fragmentary or imprecise, recipes evolved into what is today our classic French cuisine.

—Jeannette M. Seaver

For the reader's convenience, and to avoid repetition, I include below a few basic components that are used over and over throughout the book.—*Tr.*

AIOLI
2 garlic cloves, germ removed
1 large egg yolk
1 tablespoon Dijon mustard
1 tablespoon lemon juice
1 1/2 cups olive oil
pepper and salt

Put ingredients in the blender except for the oil. Turn blender on, and slowly trickle oil until mixture becomes firm. If you feel it is too thick, add a few drops water. If too thin, add 1 slice bread (crust removed), and mix in blender for a few seconds.

BOUQUET GARNI
To flavor a stock or other cooking liquid, a bunch of aromatic herbs is tied with string and immersed in the liquid. Usually the bouquet consists of a few sprigs of parsley, thyme, rosemary, bay leaves, and chives, though the composition may vary. The bundle is removed before using the stock.

CRÈME FRAICHE
In a bowl, mix 1 cup heavy cream and 2 tablespoons sour cream. Cover and let sit overnight or a bit longer. Stir the crème fraiche and refrigerate.

PÂTE BRISÉE
2 ½ cups unbleached flour
2 sticks unsalted butter, cut into pieces
1 teaspoon salt
1 teaspoon sugar
½ cup ice water

Pulse all ingredients in the food processor until it comes together. Remove from processor, and form a ball of dough with your hands. Wrap and refrigerate at least one hour.

STOCK
Stock can be made with the bones of beef, veal, chicken, or fish. Immerse the bones in a kettle of water with carrots, leeks, onion, celery, bouquet garni, peppercorns, and salt, and simmer for at least an hour, or longer for a stronger stock. Strain, discarding the solids, and refrigerate. A vegetable stock may be made without bones. For a dark stock, or *fond brun*, the bones and vegetables are roasted before simmering. Fish stock, *fumet de poisson*, is made with white wine.

Hare from the Mothers Blanc
Lièvre des mères Blanc

The department of Ain, situated at the eastern edge of France in the Rhône-Alpes region, is named after the Ain River, which divides the department's pastoral western half from the mountains of the Jura that extend east to Switzerland.

Étienne Blanc, saluting his ancestresses in his recipe title, plays on the fact that the region's foremost chef, Georges Blanc, took over a restaurant already made famous by his mother, La Mère Blanc.

"I discovered this old recipe on very yellowed, nearly transparent paper one day in my family home as I was looking at a book dating from before the Revolution. It belonged to an ancestor of mine."

Étienne Blanc
Deputy of Ain

Serves 8

1 hare, about 4–5 pounds, cut up in pieces, blood reserved
4 cups red wine
4 carrots, sliced
2 onions, finely chopped
1 bouquet garni (parsley, thyme, bay leaf, chives)
Pepper and salt
3 tablespoons butter
3 tablespoons olive oil
1 garlic clove, minced
1/3 cup balsamic vinegar
2 tablespoons flour
3 cups beef stock, from pot-au-feu (see Monday)
2 small blood sausages made with onion

BEFOREHAND:
✓ On a tray, leave hare outside in the open air, if you can, lightly covered with a thin cheesecloth, for 3–4 days. Reserve blood and giblets in the refrigerator.
MONDAY:
✓ [While I share with the Blanc family a preference for making the traditional pot-au-feu, and using its flavorful broth, these days one can find excellent ready-made beef stock in cartons or cans.—*Tr.*]
POT-AU-FEU
✓ In a large kettle, put a meaty beef shin bone, 3–4 short ribs, 2 marrow bones, 1 onion studded with 3 cloves, celery, leek, 2 carrots, and parsley. Cover meat with water all the way to the top of the kettle. Bring to a boil, reduce heat, add sea salt and peppercorns, cover, and continue cooking 1 hour, skimming now and then with a slotted spoon to remove the scum.
✓ When the meat is tender, you must sit down and enjoy the pot-au-feu with some of its rich broth. *Bon appétit!* The leftover stock will be used in the hare recipe on Thursday. Filter it through a colander. You should have at least 3–4 cups. Refrigerate.
TUESDAY:
✓ Remove and discard layer of fat formed on top of cold stock. Replace in refrigerator.
✓ In a bowl, mix wine, carrots, onions, bouquet garni, pepper, and salt. Transfer marinade into a plastic bag along with the pieces of hare. Refrigerate 24 hours.
WEDNESDAY:
✓ In a pan, heat 1 tablespoon butter and 1 tablespoon olive oil. Sauté neck, giblet, and head, with chopped carrots and onion from the marinade, and garlic clove. Cook 1 hour. Deglaze the pan with the balsamic vinegar. Reserve liver and heart.
✓ Discard the hare pieces. Press the vegetables and liquid through a sieve. Discard the solids and save the *jus.*
THURSDAY:
✓ Remove meat from marinade. Dry with absorbent paper. Filter marinade. In a heavy pot, melt the remaining 2 tablespoons butter and 2 tablespoons oil, and sauté meat until nicely golden. Sprinkle with 2 tablespoons flour, pepper and salt. Pour in the filtered marinade, 1 cup beef broth, and the reserved blood and *jus.* Stir. Cover. Cook over low heat 1 hour. Add stock as needed.
FRIDAY:
✓ Finely chop the reserved liver and the heart. Add to the meat preparation, along with the pieces of mashed blood sausage, bringing up to a simmer and stirring to incorporate well. Set aside.
SUNDAY:
✓ Bring the civet to a simmer and finish the cooking. Serve with flat noodles.

Bresse Chicken in Vin Jaune Sauce with Rutabaga Purée

Poulet de Bresse au vin jaune et purée de rutabagas au comté

With its legendary poulet *from the Bresse region and its lush woods and meadows, the department of Ain is often referred to as the farmyard of France. In 1957 the Agriculture Ministry under President Coty granted the* poulet de Bresse *the rare and coveted AOC (Appellation d'Origine Contrôlée) designation, guaranteeing its place of origin. A chicken with blue feet, it is the only fowl in the world to have received such distinction. Star of all worthy* grandes tables, *the Bresse chicken is widely exported and can be found in good American poultry shops.*

Vin jaune too is of strictly local production, a characteristic Jura wine. Its bouquet is not unlike that of sherry. In the absence of vin jaune, *one can substitute with half white wine, half sherry.*

The Comté cheese, from the same region, is a dry, rich cheese with a hint of hazelnut flavor.

"Our Michelin three-star chef, Georges Blanc, and all the fine restaurateurs of the Ain have spotlighted our star product. Here is a traditional poulet de Bresse *recipe to enjoy with—or without—moderation."*

Xavier Breton
Deputy of Ain

Serves 8

2 Bresse chickens, plucked and drawn
1 tablespoon butter
1 tablespoon olive oil
1/2 cup chopped parsley
3 tablespoons fresh thyme
1 tablespoon fresh marjoram
1 tablespoon fresh oregano
Pepper and salt
1 bottle vin jaune or Jura macvin
1 pound Comté cheese
1 cup walnuts, chopped
4 cups heavy cream
1 caul (your butcher will give you one)

For the rutabaga purée:

1 pound rutabaga, peeled and cubed
2 sticks butter
Pepper and salt

✓ Wash chickens, pat dry. Remove legs, cut them at the joint.

✓ In a pan, melt butter and oil, sauté legs until brown. Add herbs and seasonings. After 15 minutes, deglaze with wine, reserving 1 cup for the end. Continue cooking 30 minutes.

✓ Meanwhile, grate 1/2 pound of the Comté, set it aside, and cut the other 1/2 pound into cubes. Cut the breasts off the chickens and cube the meat. In a large bowl, combine cubed chicken breasts, cubed Comté, and walnuts. Add 2 cups cream, mix well.

✓ Preheat oven to 350°F.

✓ On a board, lay out the sheet of caul fat or *crépine*. Cut into 8 pieces/*crépinettes*. Place a dollop of the chicken mixture in the center of each section of *crépine* and fold it into a neat package. Set the 8 stuffed *crépinettes* in an ovenproof dish, seam side down.

✓ Bake at 350°F for 30 minutes.

✓ While the *crépinettes* are baking, start the rutabaga (below).

✓ When chicken legs are cooked, remove and keep warm. Strain the sauce into a saucepan, reheating while stirring in the remaining 2 cups heavy cream. Gently stir in the 1/2 pound grated cheese until it melts and thickens the sauce. Keep sauce warm, and stir in remaining 1 cup wine.

RUTABAGA

✓ In a pot half filled with boiling, salted water, cook rutabaga for 20 minutes. Drain. Purée in the food processor or mash by hand, incorporating all the butter. Season to taste.

Place one crépinette *along with a half chicken leg on each plate. Add a dollop of rutabaga purée. Coat with the sauce, and serve.*

Maroilles Cheese Tart

Tarte au maroilles

The two deputies from the Aisne department—whose name comes from the most central of its three main rivers—have agreed to jointly contribute the same traditional recipe. This tarte is prepared with a pâte levée, a yeasty dough characteristic of the region. Its main ingredient, the Maroilles cheese, has been produced for centuries in Thiérache, the vast region bordering Belgium, and takes its name from the village of Maroilles in the Nord department just adjacent to Aisne. Square, with a perfectly edible smooth pink skin, Maroilles is a soft cow's-milk cheese that imparts a strong flavor.

The tarte aux maroilles is served hot as the main part of the meal, savored with a green salad. This recipe was prepared by Xavier Bertrand and Isebelle Vasseur, deputies of Aisne.

✔ Preheat oven to 450°F.

✔ In a small cup, put yeast sprinkled with a little sugar. Add warm milk. Wait a few minutes until it becomes foamy. In a bowl, mix yeast mixture with flour and salt. Add eggs and butter. Knead 2 minutes until it becomes elastic and smooth. Cover. Let rise 1 hour.

✔ Punch risen dough down, roll it out, and line a tart mold with it. Let rise another 30 minutes.

✔ Scrape skin of Maroilles without removing it. Cut in thin slices. Line pie dough with cheese slices. In the food processor, blend yolks and crème fraiche until smooth. Cover cheese with the mixture.

✔ Bake 30 minutes.

<u>Serves 6</u>

For the dough:

1 envelope dry yeast

Pinch of sugar

1/4 cup warm milk

1 1/2 cups unbleached flour

1/2 teaspoon salt

2 eggs

4 tablespoons butter, softened

For the filling:

1 Maroilles cheese

2 egg yolks

6 ounces crème fraiche

1/4 teaspoon fresh pepper

Potato and Cream Pâté

Pâté bourbonnais aux pommes de terre

"The pâté bourbonnais? A very local recipe in every way—its name, its ingredients, the know-how necessary to make it, and especially what it is: un rien trublion, *a little troublemaker. As was considered the old province of the Bourbonnais, the land now called the Allier, from early on was regarded as unruly by the government of the Auvergne, which tried to annihilate it, unsuccessfully.*

"The pâté bourbonnais is like that, mutinous. It goes against all the traditions of the culinary canon. Potatoes? Encased in pastry? And flooded with heavy cream? Such an unlikely union. Yet all who taste it are won over.

"Another confirmation of its local authenticity is that it is best eaten only with other products of the Bourbonnais. The rougette or doucette lettuce grown in the mud of the Allier banks, or the ham air-dried in our Bourbonnais mountains, and of course the white Auvergne wine of Saint-Pourçain—a unique cépage that balances perfectly the richness of our pâté.

"Omit or add any ingredient at your own risk. Beware of turning our pâté into a most improbable pudding!"

Gérard Charasse
Deputy of Allier

"The potato pâté was born in the farming country between Target and Voussac in the Allier in 1789, a time of great food shortage. In those days the farmers, all observing the religious rules strictly, never ate meat on Fridays. To add to the privation, they were not permitted to fish the ponds in the woodlands belonging to their Bourbon overlords. What were they to do?

"With the few components they were able to scare up, they devised a new Friday meal consisting of a potato-filled two-crust pie, cooked without liquid and then infused with crème fraîche, an ingredient all farms had in good supply.

"This pâté bourbonnais has survived the years, and today many bakeries in the region as well as local restaurants offer the potato pâté every Friday."

Jean Mallot
Deputy of Allier

"Among the excellent recipes from the Auvergne, the most ubiquitous in the Allier is without doubt this very pâté. All three of us agree that our pâté bourbonnais represents the best that our region has to offer. This is the gourmet version, although some who incline more toward gourmand may add ham, or even turn it into a dessert by substituting pears."

Bernard Lesterlin
Deputy of Allier

✔ Preheat oven to 350°F.

✔ In a bowl, with your fingers, mix flour, oil, water, and salt until it forms a homogeneous dough. Do not overmix. You may wish to add either a few more drops of water, if it appears too dry, or some more flour or oil. The more oil, the more unctuous the dough will be.

✔ Divide dough into two equal balls. On a floured work surface, roll out the first ball and place it in a 10-inch pie plate, letting extra dough hang over sides.

✔ In a bowl, mix potatoes with onions, herbs, nutmeg, pepper, and salt. Place potato slices in a circular array in the piecrust, making sure to have more slices in the middle.

✔ Roll out the second ball of dough and place over potatoes. Crimp the two crusts together to seal the pie. With a knife, cut out a cross in the middle and fold back the four corners to create a chimney. For decorative effect, make light incisions all around. In a small bowl, lightly beat the egg yolk with 2 tablespoons water. Brush top of pie with this egg wash. Bake 45–60 minutes.

✔ Remove from oven. Cut out a circle in the middle of the crust and pour the cream inside, poking with a knife and tilting the pie to distribute the cream as best you can. (A little messy, but worth it.) Replace the circle. Serve hot, warm, or cold.

Serves 6

For the crust:

3 cups unbleached flour

1/2 cup olive oil

6 tablespoons cold water

1/2 teaspoon salt

For the filling:

2 pounds potatoes, peeled and cut into thin slices

1 large onion, minced

1/4 cup chives, finely chopped

1/2 cup parsley, finely chopped

1/2 cup chervil, finely chopped

1/4 teaspoon freshly ground nutmeg

Freshly ground pepper

Pinch of fleur de sel

1 cup plus 2 tablespoons heavy cream

1 egg yolk

Lamb's Feet and Stomach Parcels, Sisteron Style

Pieds et paquets

Feet and stomachs. Perhaps off-putting, for non-French gourmands? Once you get past the literal translation, however, and taste the dish, you will agree that it is savory, and unique. Pieds et paquets happens to be among the finest, most delicate dishes in Provence's cuisine. Like so many in French gastronomy, it was born out of poverty, long ago, when meat was rare and literally every animal part had to be used. This recipe is not for the faint of heart. It also requires that you enjoy a good relationship with your butcher. The secret for making this traditional specialty is cooking it for seven hours. A tip from Sisteron chefs is to prepare the dish the day before.

"This recipe comes from Mr. Jacques Guistini, butcher-charcutier in Sisteron. It is made with the Red Label lamb—a distinction awarded by the government guaranteeing that the lamb is of local origin and pasture-fed. A great many natives of Sisteron take pride in preparing the traditional specialty. It is so much a part of their culture that each year Sisteron holds a Concours des Pieds et Paquets, with prizes, inviting amateurs to compete along with professionals. Mr. Guistini has won first prize several times."

Daniel Spagnou
Deputy of Alpes-de-Haute-Provence

Serves 6

6 lamb's feet
1 lamb stomach
1 cup parsley, finely chopped
2 garlic cloves, minced
1/4 pound pork belly, ground in the food processor
Pepper and salt
1/4 cup olive oil
1 onion, finely chopped
5 carrots, sliced
2 pounds tomatoes, peeled, with juice (canned is fine)
1/3 cup tomato paste
1 veal foot
1 bouquet garni
2 cloves garlic, minced
2 bottles white wine
2 pounds potatoes, peeled
1/2 cup parsley, finely chopped

✓ Make sure the feet have been well cleaned by your butcher.

✓ In a kettle, bring 4 quarts of water to a boil. Reduce heat, cook lamb stomach 30 minutes. Drain. Cut into 6 pieces.

✓ In a bowl, mix parsley, garlic, pork belly, pepper and salt. Place 2 tablespoons of stuffing on each of the stomach pieces. Roll into a parcel. It will look like a sausage.

✓ In a large, heavy-bottomed casserole or Dutch oven, heat the oil. Sauté onion and carrots. Add tomatoes, tomato paste, veal foot, bouquet garni, and garlic. Pour wine in, and stir. When it comes to a boil, add the lamb parcels and feet. Cover and reduce heat to a simmer. After 2 hours, remove lamb's feet and set aside (otherwise they would be overcooked). Continue to cook for another 5 hours. Stir now and then, making sure nothing sticks. For the last 30 minutes, put the lamb's feet back in. Taste and adjust the seasoning.

✓ In a separate pot, boil potatoes for 20 minutes. Drain. Sprinkle with parsley.

✓ With a slotted spoon, remove the *pieds et paquets* and place on a serving platter along with the potatoes. Strain the cooking liquid, pressing the solids through the sieve to produce a velvety sauce. Serve.

Two-Cheese Quenelles
Moines

In French gastronomy, you are likely to find dishes, as well as many cheeses, bearing clerical titles. Love of the Church? Love that equals love of food? Gallic humor?
"This recipe has been given to me by the chef of La Neyrette in Saint-Disdier-en-Dévoluy. These 'monks' are merely quenelles (dumplings) rolled by hand, deep fried, and presented on a chiffonade of salad drizzled with a coulis of shallots and honey."

Henriette Martinez
Deputy of Hautes-Alpes

Serves 15

For the "Moine"/quenelles:

2 pounds potatoes, peeled, cooked, and pressed through a ricer

4 eggs

2 cups cottage cheese

1 cup grated Gruyère cheese

1 1/2 tablespoons baking powder

Pepper and salt

6 cups flour, approximately

Oil for frying

For the coulis:

1 pound shallots

2 cups raspberry vinegar

3 cups honey

For the salad:

1 head Boston lettuce, leaves washed and dried

2 tablespoons raspberry vinegar

5 tablespoons walnut oil

✓ In a bowl, combine potatoes, eggs, cottage cheese, Gruyère, baking powder, pepper and salt. Mix well. Add flour gradually. When mixture is well integrated and still soft, form little finger-size sausages. Place them in the freezer to firm them.

✓ In a pan, over medium heat, cook shallots in vinegar until vinegar has evaporated. Stir in honey and keep warm.

✓ In a bowl, place the salad, finely shredded. In a cup mix 2 tablespoons raspberry vinegar, 5 tablespoons walnut oil, pepper and salt. Toss the salad with the dressing. Divide equally among plates.

✓ In a deep pot, heat the frying oil, not too hot. Remove quenelles from freezer. Drop a few quenelles in the oil, cook until crisp on all sides. Remove and drain on absorbent paper. Repeat until all quenelles are fried.

✓ Arrange the quenelles on the chiffonade, drizzle with the honey coulis, and serve.

Sheep Cheese and Potato Pastries

Tourtons du Champsaur "maison" à la tomme de brebis

"The tourtons come from the Valley of Champsaur, near Gap, and were first made in the nineteenth century. In those days the cultivation of the potato was Champsaur's main activity and the inspiration for these small fried dough 'pillows' filled with cheese and mashed potatoes. Part of the traditional Christmas Eve menu, they were called coussins du petit Jésus—*Little Jesus' pillows. Each Champsaur family had its own unique recipe, a closely guarded secret passed down the generations. Today, however,* tourtons *are served throughout the country, and with a wide variety of fillings."*

Joël Giraud
Deputy of Hautes-Alpes

✓ In the food processor, blend flour, 1 teaspoon salt, and shortening coarsely, then add the egg and 4 tablespoons warm water and pulse until dough is formed. Refrigerate while preparing the filling.

✓ Peel and cook potatoes. Drain. In a bowl, mash or rice the potatoes, adding enough milk to make a thick purée. Mix in the sheep cheese, nutmeg, and a little salt to taste.

✓ On a lightly floured work surface, roll out dough very thin. Cut into 4-by-2-inch rectangles. (A serrated or fluted wheel cutter works well.) Place a spoonful of filling on one end of each rectangle, leaving a border. Moisten the border, fold the dough over, and press to seal the dough all around.

✓ Heat the oil in a deep kettle, and fry *tourtons* 3 minutes on each side. Drain on absorbent paper. Repeat until all are fried. Serve.

Serves 12

1 3/4 cup unbleached flour
1 teaspoon salt
5 tablespoons shortening
1 egg
1/2 pound potatoes
1/4 cup milk
2 ounces well-aged sheep cheese, diced
1/2 teaspoon freshly grated nutmeg
1 quart peanut oil for frying

Chickpea Galette
Socca

"Socca is a thin, crisp, delicious pancake-like flatbread made of chickpea flour. Invented in Genoa, socca crossed the border long ago, and somehow the city of Nice seems to have appropriated it as its own specialty. You see vendors throughout the city baking it in small, portable wood-fire ovens in their trucks, and selling the freshly made socca in paper cones. An all-day snack, it also serves as appetizer base or is eaten, like bread, with any meal. Part and parcel of Nice restaurants and all eateries, socca is a Nice emblem."

Éric Ciotti
Deputy of Alpes-Maritimes

Serves 4

1 cup chickpea flour, sifted
1 cup lukewarm water
1 teaspoon salt
1 teaspoon black pepper
1/2 teaspoon cumin
1 teaspoon rosemary
6 tablespoons olive oil

✓ Preheat oven to 450°F.
✓ Put skillet in the oven until it is blazing hot.
✓ Meanwhile, in a bowl, mix flour, water, salt, pepper, cumin, and rosemary into a loose batter.
✓ Put 1 or 2 tablespoons olive oil in hot skillet, pour batter in, swirl to cover. Bake 15 minutes until it becomes blistery and edges are getting brown. You may, if you wish, put it under the broiler for 1 minute at this point to achieve a darker, crisper look. Drizzle with a little olive oil, salt, and serve. Repeat until batter is all used.

Roasted Red Peppers in Olive Oil

Poivrons grillés

"Born in Paris, I discovered the wonderful roasted peppers as a child during my vacations on the Côtes d'Azur. They were a revelation for me, something we didn't eat at home. I later moved south and married a native of Cannes. This recipe comes from her Provençal cuisine."

Lionnel Luca
Deputy of Alpes-Maritimes

Serves 6–8
8 red peppers, washed and dried, whole
2 garlic cloves, minced
Pepper and salt
1/2 cup olive oil

✔ Preheat oven to 450°F. Line a baking sheet with foil and roast peppers 30 minutes, turning them occasionally with tongs. When the skin is charred, turn off the oven and let them finish cooking.
✔ Peel under running cold water. Remove seeds. Cut in strips and arrange in a serving platter or a bowl. Sprinkle peppers with garlic, salt and pepper, and drizzle with olive oil. Cover with plastic wrap and refrigerate a few hours. Serve.

For visual effect, you may mix peppers of different colors. Roasting during summer, when peppers are fully ripe, makes for a typical and delicious first course or lunch fare.

Pie of Swiss Chard, Apples, Pine Nuts, Raisins, and Cheese

Tourta de bléa

"I chose this recipe because it truly belongs to the Nice patrimony, and because it reminds me of the Sundays of my childhood, when my mother used to prepare it for dessert. As often friends joined us, my father liked to open a good Bellet rosé wine (granted AOC status in 1941) from one of the oldest vineyards of France, to accompany the tourta."

Muriel Marland-Militello
Deputy of Alpes-Maritimes

✓ Place all the dough ingredients in the food processor and pulse, adding a few tablespoons of water if needed, until mixture comes together and forms a dough—about 5 minutes. Refrigerate while preparing the filling.

✓ In a large bowl, set the two kinds of raisins to soak in the rum.

✓ Stack the Swiss chard leaves, slice finely, and wash in several changes of cold water until the water no longer turns green (this removes the bitterness). Squeeze the chard dry and stir it into the rum-raisin marinade. Leave for 1 hour or more.

✓ Drain the rum off the chard and raisins. Reserve rum. To the bowl of chard and raisins, add eggs, brown sugar, Parmesan, pine nuts, liquor, olive oil, and salt. If mixture appears too dry, add a few drops of the rum.

✓ Preheat oven to 375°F. Butter and flour the inside of a deep pie plate or cake pan.

✓ On a floured work surface, divide dough equally. Roll out both halves. Line cake pan with one. Add the solid part of the filling, to a depth of about 1 inch, and moisten it with half its juice. Top completely with apple slices, thinly cut. Cover with second circle of dough, pinching it sealed with your fingers. With a fork, prick little holes on top.

✓ Bake 45 minutes or until pie looks golden brown and edges begin to pull away from the pan. Remove from oven. Sprinkle with white sugar. Serve.

Serves 8

For the dough:

3 cups flour

1 egg

1/2 pound butter (2 sticks), cut in small pieces

1 1/2 cups sugar, preferably superfine

1/4 teaspoon salt

For the filling:

3 tablespoons dark raisins

3 tablespoons golden raisins

2/3 cup rum

4 pounds Swiss chard leaves (without stems) washed free of sand

2 eggs

1 cup brown sugar

1/2 cup grated Parmesan or dry mountain cheese

1/2 cup pine nuts

1/4 cup eau-de-vie or brandy

1 tablespoon olive oil

1/4 teaspoon salt

2–3 apples

Baked Eggs with Morels
Oeufs cocotte aux morilles

A tributary of the Rhône, the Ardèche River rises in the Cévennes and flows southeast across the department that bears its name. Its final thirty kilometers, the Gorges de l'Ardèche, are regarded as the largest natural canyon in Europe. The limestone cliffs are dotted with caves that exhibit signs of prehistoric life, including the Chauvet–Pont d'Arc Grotto with extraordinary drawings from the Upper Paleolithic era.

"Because the best things are often the simplest, I find myself relying on this dish as a first course when I entertain. Varieties of mushrooms abound in the Ardèche—cèpes (porcini), chanterelles, morels, milkcaps—each in season imparting an exceptional flavor. Here morels contribute a most delicate touch to this otherwise classic recipe."

Jean-Claude Flory
Deputy of Ardèche

Serves 6

1 cup morels or other mushrooms
2 tablespoons butter
1/2 cup heavy cream, preferably crème fraiche
1/2 cup grated Gruyère
1/2 cup diced ham
Freshly ground pepper
6 eggs, at room temperature
6 slices white or whole wheat bread

✓ If using dry morels, reconstitute in water for 2 hours, squeeze dry, and chop.

✓ Preheat oven to 350°F. Fill a baking dish one-third full of water. Butter 6 four-inch ramekins and place in baking dish.

✓ In a bowl, mix heavy cream, ham, and morels. Divide among ramekins. In each, make a well in the center of the cream mixture and break an egg into it. Top with freshly ground pepper.

✓ Bake for about 20 minutes, or until the white of the egg is set, while the yolk remains soft.

✓ Meanwhile toast the bread and cut it into fingers or *mouillettes*. Serve with the baked eggs.

Cream of Chestnut Soup
Cousina

"Chestnuts are an integral part of French gastronomy, and chestnuts from the Ardèche represent half the national production. Chestnut cultivation, processing, and exporting contribute greatly to our economy. Emblematic of our department, the chestnut is our identity and our patrimony. Infinite care and pride are given to all aspects of its production, especially since the government recently awarded the AOC designation to our châtaignes d'Ardèche.

"This versatile autumn fruit lends itself to a variety of presentations. Fresh chestnuts in the shell are roasted. Chestnuts can be dried, like mushrooms. Whole chestnuts, fresh or canned, are enjoyed in stuffings. In purée—also available canned—they make a savory accompaniment to all kinds of roasted meat or fowl. As dessert, the delicate purée is served with crème fraiche. And then there is the famous crème de marrons, different in texture and flavor from the purée, that appears in the dessert called Mont Blanc, also with crème fraiche. French children spread crème de marrons on bread, as American children do with peanut butter, for their goûter or afternoon snack. Finally, chestnut flour may be used by those allergic to gluten."

Pascal Terrasse
Deputy of Ardèche

Serves 6

2 pounds fresh chestnuts, or 1 1/2 pounds already peeled
4 cups chicken stock
6 celery leaves
1/2 teaspoon nutmeg
Pepper and salt
4 cups heavy cream

✓ If using chestnuts in the shell, make a cross with a sharp knife on the flat side of each chestnut. In a kettle, bring 2 quarts water to a boil. Cook 5 minutes. With a slotted spoon, remove one chestnut at a time and peel. Keep the remaining ones in hot water to facilitate peeling.

✓ In a heavy-bottomed saucepan, heat chicken stock with celery leaves, nutmeg, pepper, and salt. Pass one-third of the chestnuts through a ricer, add them to the stock, and cook for 30 minutes.

✓ Stir in crème fraiche, bring back up to heat, and add the remaining two-thirds of the peeled chestnuts. Simmer for 1 hour. Adjust seasoning, and serve.

[Personally, I recommend buying peeled and cooked chestnuts. You'll need 3–4 jars. Cook already cooked chestnuts in flavored stock for 8 minutes. Pass through ricer. Return to kettle. Stir in heavy cream. Serve.—*Tr.*]

Serve with a red Côtes-du-Vivarais.

Cooked Wilted Salad with Lardons and Fingerling Potatoes

Salade au lard ardennaise

The Ardennes department takes its name from the forested highlands that extend from the northeast of France into Belgium and Luxembourg. The strategic position of the Ardennes made it a battleground for European powers for centuries, culminating in World War II's Battle of the Bulge.

"Salad with bacon is the Ardennes specialty. It is said that there are as many variants of this salad as there are inhabitants of the Ardennes. This is mine."

Bérangère Poletti
Deputy of Ardennes

Serves 6

24 fingerling potatoes
2 tablespoons cooking oil
1 bunch dandelion greens, or
1 escarole, washed, dried, and chopped
1 onion, diced
1 shallot, minced
1 garlic clove, minced
6 thick slices bacon, diced
1/2 cup wine vinegar
Pepper and salt

✓ Cook potatoes in their skins. Peel and roughly smash.

✓ In a heavy-bottomed pot, heat 1 tablespoon oil and throw in the salad greens. When they have cooked down for a few minutes and are nicely wilted, throw in the shallot, onion, garlic, and smashed potatoes. Do not stir.

✓ In a skillet, fry the bacon bits (lardons). Spread them over the potato bed. Deglaze bacon pan with vinegar. Pour liquid over potato. Do not stir. Cover and cook 5 minutes over low heat.

✓ Now, and not before, stir potato mixture. Cover again and continue cooking over low heat for 30 minutes, stirring regularly.

✓ Serve hot, alone as the main dish, or with a fried egg or a pork chop.

"This Ardennes specialty tastes even better when reheated, so make a big potful and plan on leftovers. While it is clearly not haute cuisine, it is delicious comfort food—just a couple of good ingredients along with a good dose of gourmandise."

Fricassée of Potatoes with Bacon

Cacasse à cul nu

The term cacasse *is a truncated version of "fricassée of potatoes."* Nu *here stands for "peeled." Literally: "potatoes with naked bottoms."*

"Like many recipes from rural France, cacasse à cul nu *emanates from a time of extreme poverty in the Ardennes. No meat was to be had, and this dish represented the full meal. Only at the beginning of the month when people felt 'rich' did they add a bit of bacon. Despite its apparent simplicity, it is savory and delicious.*

"At a time when Parmentier was still proselytizing the new vegetable to Parisian chefs at the royal court, the papal legate had brought potato sprouts with him to Belgium. Soon the troeff *(potato, in patois) had found its way across the border and started to grow in the French Ardennes' vegetable gardens. The Ardennais, known never to hesitate when faced with something tasty, embraced the new arrival—and so did their pigs, who took voraciously to the potatoes, making their ham all the better. Like the* salade au lard *in the previous recipe, this* cacasse *soon became a culinary emblem of the Ardennes region."*

Philippe Vuilque
Deputy of Ardennes

✓ In a heavy-bottomed pot, cook bacon slices until nearly crisp. Remove and reserve. Add oil and onions, and cook until golden brown. Stir in flour to obtain a lightly browned roux, then 1 cup water. Add potatoes, thyme, bay leaf, pepper, salt, and more water to cover by 1/2 inch. Cover and simmer for about 45 minutes. Test the potatoes and, 10 minutes before serving, top with bacon slices.

"In the Ardennes, cacasse is mostly eaten by itself, but you may serve it with pork or sausages, or with chicken breast cooked along with the potatoes. A fresh green salad is always a welcome accompaniment."

Serves 6
1/2 pound thick bacon slices
1/4 cup olive oil
2 large onions, finely chopped
2 tablespoons flour
3 pounds potatoes, peeled and quartered
1 teaspoon thyme
1 bay leaf
Pepper and salt

Cabbage Soup with Smoked Pork and Sausage

Asinat ariégeois

The Ariège department in southwestern France shares a border with both Spain and Andorra. Villages dating from before the Middle Ages were built on its rocky Pyrénées slopes where little was able to grow. Poverty was supreme.

"Asinat, the hearty cabbage soup of the Ariège, is one of those traditional peasant dishes produced by resourceful grandmothers—fixtures in almost every farmer's home—who would stay bent over an ever-burning wood fire, stirring patiently for hours until their sons and husbands returned for supper, hungry, after a long hard day.

"The asinat, with its slow cooking time and its infusion of flavor from rinds and remains of previous pork dishes, acquires a deep, smoky, seasoned aroma that transforms it from a simple dish into one worthy of a feast.

"If there are leftovers the next day, mash the solids into croquettes, drizzle with a few drops of olive oil, and bake in a moderate oven until crisp.

"Asinat continues to be served today in the Ariège, thanks to yesterday's little girls who, having become grandmothers, perpetuate our tradition."

Henri Nayrou
Deputy of Ariège

Serves 6–8

1 white cabbage, cut into quarters
2 tablespoons duck fat
1 onion, minced
2 garlic cloves, smashed
2 tablespoons flour
6 carrots, peeled and cut into thick pieces
4 chunky pieces of pork (cutlets, or cut pieces of pork roast)
3 pieces of pork rind
1 small dry pork sausage
1 small ham hock
Pepper and salt
16 potatoes, peeled and halved
4 slices stale bread

✓ In a kettle, bring 2 quarts salted water to a boil. Cook cabbage 5 minutes. Drain. Set aside.

✓ In a large soup pot or Dutch oven, heat duck fat, cook onion until cleared. Add garlic, stir in flour, and slowly add 1 cup water to form a sauce. Add carrots, cabbage, pork products, pepper, and salt. Pour water to 2 inches above meat and vegetables. Cover. Over very low heat, simmer 1 1/2 hours. Add potatoes, cover again, and cook 20 minutes more.

✓ Remove the meats and vegetables to a serving platter. Keep warm.

✓ Place bread slices at the bottom of a soup tureen. Add broth. Serve the soup first, followed by the meats and vegetables.

Salmon Steamed over Cabbage

Saumon servi avec son chou

The Aube department in northeastern France, watered by both the River Aube and the Seine, was created in 1790 from the former province of Champagne. In 1919, by a new decree, Aube wine producers were authorized to produce champagne along with their northern neighbors in the Marne department. This recipe was prepared by Nicolas Dhuicq, deputy of Aube.

Serves 4

2 cups choucroute, prepared or homemade (recipe below)
4 salmon filets
Pepper and salt
1 tablespoon lumpfish caviar
1 cup chives, finely chopped

For homemade choucroute:

3 tablespoons duck fat
1 onion, finely chopped
1 small cabbage, thinly shredded
8 juniper berries
Pepper
1 1/2 cups chicken stock
1 cup dry white wine

✓ If making your own choucroute, this is a shortcut: heat the duck fat in a skillet and sauté onion until golden. Add cabbage, juniper berries, pepper. Sauté 5 more minutes. Stir in stock and wine. Cover and simmer 1 hour or more, stirring occasionally, adding more liquid as needed.

✓ If using prepared choucroute, rinse under running water and squeeze dry. Put choucroute in the bottom of a steamer and evenly lay salmon in the upper section. Cover. Turn heat on, and cook 10 minutes, without turning salmon over—this cooking method, called *à l'unilatéral*, leaves the fish moist and tender.

✓ Divide choucroute among warmed plates, place salmon on top. Add pepper and salt to taste, and sprinkle with lumpfish caviar and chives. Serve.

Castelnaudary Cassoulet
Cassoulet de Castelnaudary

"Cassoulet is a long Aude tradition.

"Known for two thousand years for its rich wine production, Aude's rich gastronomy has been dominated by its famous cassoulet—emblematic of Castelnaudary since the Middle Ages.

"According to legend, during a British siege of Castelnaudary in the Hundred Years War in the fifteenth century, as the French soldiers were threatened by starvation, the townspeople rallied, pooling every item of food they could put their hands on—pork, meats, sausages, bacon, fava beans—which they cooked in a big cauldron. The soldiers of Castelnaudary, reinvigorated by this cassoulet, apparently pushed the British invaders out of the Languedoc and all the way to the English Channel.

"Here the legend stops.

"Cassoulet as we know it today settled firmly into French cuisine in the early sixteenth century when haricots lingots, *regular white beans, made their entry into Europe, replacing fava beans in the cassoulet.*

"The first industrial cassoulet company was founded in Castelnaudary in 1836, and the city became the capital of cassoulet, with a yearly celebration welcoming thousands of participants, chefs and consumers alike."

Jean-Paul Dupré
Deputy of Aude

✓ In a bowl or pot, cover beans with ample water and let soak for 3 hours.

✓ Meanwhile, score the skin of the duck and roast at 300°F for 2 hours. Cut into pieces. Reserve the rendered fat.

✓ In the food processor, grind garlic, salt pork, and ham to make the *hachis*.

✓ In a large pot half full of water, place the pork rind, *hachis*, and pepper and salt, and cook 30 minutes. Add thyme, bay leaf, and drained beans. Continue cooking 30 minutes. Beans should be tender.

✓ In a pan, heat duck fat and sauté pork loin until nicely brown. Remove and slice. Add sausages, cook 10 minutes, and remove. If using prepared confit, brown the duck pieces as well. Season all the meats. Deglaze the pan with a little water and add it to the beans.

✓ Rub the bottom of a large baking pan or glazed earthenware baking dish with garlic, and grind pepper over it. Add rind, a layer of beans, duck, pork, sausages, ending with another layer of beans. Bake 1 1/2 hours at 350°F. You might add some stock if it appears dry. You'll see a crust form and a slight bubbling of the beans. Serve.

Serves 12–15

3 cups dried white beans

1 duck, or equivalent amount of confit de canard

3 pork rinds

Pepper and salt

1 teaspoon thyme

1 bay leaf

1 small loin of pork, 4–5 pounds

2 pounds smoked sausage, such as kielbasa

1 garlic clove, peeled and halved

For the hachis:

2 heads garlic, peeled

1 pound salt pork

1 1/2 pounds ham

Flan in a Pie Crust
Flaune aveyronnaise

The mountainous Aveyron department is situated in south-central France, at the southern edge of the Massif Central, in the region called Midi-Pyrénées.
"Flaune, the Aveyron's signature dessert, is a pie with a flan filling, made from sheep's milk ricotta, or recuite. Since the recuite is produced by recooking the buttermilk left over after Roquefort production, it can be found only in the Aveyron. In July–August, when the milking season has ended but the ewes' milk has not yet dried up, the farmers' wives use it to make a raw cheese as well as recuite for these pastries."

Alain Marc
Deputy of Aveyron

Serves 6
1 cup sheep ricotta
1 cup buttermilk
3/4 cup sugar
3 tablespoons orange flower water
1 egg, plus 5 egg yolks
1 cup crème fraiche
1 sheet puff pastry

✓ Preheat oven to 400°F.
✓ In a bowl, mash ricotta, buttermilk, and crème fraiche with sugar, orange flower water, egg, and yolks, mixing well with each addition. Beat together for a further 2 minutes.
✓ Line a 9-inch pie plate with puff pastry. With a fork, poke a few holes. Prebake 10 minutes. Remove from oven. Reduce temperature to 350°F. Pour filling onto puff pastry. Bake about 30 minutes, until filling has puffed up and begun to brown.
✓ Serve warm or cold.

Mashed Stockfish and Potatoes
Estofinado

"The stockfish is a dried, unsalted cod. Unlike its southern, Mediterranean counterpart brandade de morue, *also prepared with cod, but with salt cod,* estofinado *represents a kind of link between Norway (the Lofoten Islands) and the heart of Massif Central, the Lot Valley."*

Marie-Lou Marcel
Deputy of Aveyron

Serves 4

4 pounds dried cod, preferably not salted
1 pound potatoes, scrubbed and quartered
1/4 teaspoon salt
5 garlic cloves, minced
1 bunch parsley, finely chopped
5 hard-boiled eggs, peeled and diced
1 1/4 cups walnut oil
5 eggs, lightly beaten
10 ounces heavy cream, preferably crème fraiche
Pepper and salt

✔ Cut up fish, cover with water, and soak for 6 days, changing water twice a day.
✔ In a heavy-bottomed pot, cover fish with fresh water, bring to a boil, reduce heat, and cook 20 minutes. Lift out fish with a slotted spoon. Remove skin and bones. Flake fish with a fork. Reserve.
✔ Cook potatoes with salt in the fish water, 15–20 minutes. Drain.
✔ In the same pot, smash potatoes with a fork. Add fish, hard-boiled eggs, garlic, and parsley.
✔ In a small pan, heat the oil. Incorporate the hot oil, bit by bit, into the fish mixture, alternating with the beaten eggs. Add the crème fraiche, and season to taste.
✔ Serve very hot, with toast.

Beef Stew Provençal

Daube provençale

Daube is a beef stew prepared like boeuf bourgignon, with red wine.

"It is not necessary to marinate the meat—a method used in bygone days to tenderize the beef. Once fully prepared, the daube can be refrigerated. The gelatin from the pig's foot will solidify it so that, in summertime, it can be served in slices, like a pâté."

Christian Kert
Deputy of Bouches-du-Rhône

✔ In a skillet, heat olive oil. Sauté onion, leek, and carrot. Add beef and brown well on all sides.
✔ Line a Dutch oven with the rind. Add pig's foot, vegetables, and meat. Pour in the wine. Add orange zest, bouquet garni, tomato paste, and seasoning. Cover and simmer 3 hours.
✔ Fresh noodles, steamed potatoes, or polenta would be a good accompaniment.

Serves 6

1/3 cup olive oil
1 onion, sliced
1 leek, white only, sliced
3 carrots, sliced
3 pounds beef cheek or, if not available, chuck
1 pig's foot, split in half
2 long strips pork rind
1 bottle red wine
Zest of 1 orange
Bouquet garni
1 tablespoon tomato paste
Pepper and salt

Cod and Vegetables with Aioli

Cabillaud et légumes à l'aïoli

"This typical Provençal dish inevitably brings me back to my childhood, to our special, wonderful Friday dinners.

"In the language of Provence, the two words ail *(garlic) and* oli *(oil) suffice to describe the legendary sauce celebrated by the poet Frédéric Mistral, who in 1891 founded a newspaper he called l'Aïoli. In Mistral's words, 'Aioli in its essence conveys the warmth, the strength, the gaiety of our Provençal sun. Not to mention its other virtue—that of chasing flies away. To those whose stomachs rebel at the mere notion of our garlic and our olive oil: do not trouble yourselves to come our way.'*

"Aioli is a rich and aromatic sauce, and represents a full meal in itself, called le grand aïoli*—poached cod and a variety of vegetables served with the garlic mayonnaise.*

"By the freshness, simplicity, and excellence of its ingredients, aioli sings the art of living well."

Richard Mallié
Deputy of Bouches-du-Rhône

Serves 4

2 pounds cod
6 potatoes, sliced
1 cauliflower, separated into florets
12 carrots, whole, peeled
Handful of green beans, whole, trimmed
6 hard-boiled eggs, peeled and halved lengthwise

For the aioli:

4–6 garlic cloves, minced
1 egg yolk
Pepper and salt
1 1/2 cup olive oil

✓ Poach cod 45 minutes. Or cook in oven, wrapped tightly in foil.

✓ Meanwhile, boil potatoes, and steam or boil cauliflower, carrots, and beans just until al dente.

✓ In a bowl, mash garlic with the egg yolk, pepper, and salt. Drizzle the oil in slowly, beating steadily, until the aioli becomes thick. (Is easily made in the blender as well.) Keep refrigerated until serving.

✓ On a serving platter, present the fish surrounded by the hard-boiled eggs, potatoes, and vegetables. Pass the aioli separately.

✓ This dish can be served as soon as it has finished cooking, but it is delicious cold as well. You can of course add different vegetables.

Traditional Provençal Bean and Vegetable Soup with Pesto

Soupe au pistou

"The soupe au pistou, *integral part of our long history, becomes a matter of personal identity for us in Provence. It evokes the sun shining over our table, lighting up each guest, its rich taste reflecting the wide variety of our local bounty.*

"Each Provençal home chef guards his or her recipe as a secret, insisting it is the one.

"At the end of summer, the soupe au pistou *seems to combine sunshine and Provence in a plate, bringing back warmer days."*

Bernard Reynes
Deputy of Bouches-du-Rhône

13

Serves 8

1 pound white or red beans, soaked overnight and cooked 40 minutes

1 pound green beans, trimmed and cut in 1-inch pieces

3 small zucchinis, cubed

3 tomatoes, diced

3 potatoes, peeled and cubed

2 large onions, sliced

1 bay leaf

Pepper and salt

1/2 pound bow tie pasta

For the pistou:

6 garlic cloves

1 large bunch basil

1 cup Parmesan cheese, grated

1/2 cup olive oil

✓ In a large kettle, combine all vegetables. Cover with water. Add bay leaf, pepper, and salt. Bring to a boil, reduce heat, and simmer.

✓ After 1 hour, add the pasta. Turn heat off. Cover. Let sit 5 minutes.

✓ In a mortar or food processor, mash garlic with basil, cheese, and olive oil.

✓ Serve, with a dollop of pistou in each soup plate.

Rock Lobster à l'Américaine

Langoustes à l'américaine

Legend has it that this recipe dates from 1860, when chef Pierre Fraisse, who had just returned from America, opened his restaurant in Paris. One late evening as he was about to close, some people wandered in for dinner. The only food left in his icebox was a few lobsters. Because he produced the dinner in minutes, and because the speed reminded him of his experiences in America, on the spot, he named his lobster dish à l'Américaine. In France, blue or brown lobsters are called homard. *Those without a claw, and red, are* langouste, *rock lobster or spiny lobster.*

"This old family recipe is often made for our Christmas dinner. But it is always appreciated on all occasions."

Dominique Tian
Deputy of Bouches-du-Rhône

✓ In a kettle, bring water and bouquet garni to a boil. Cook lobsters 5 minutes. Remove from water. With a sharp knife, cut lobsters in half lengthwise. Remove roe (coral) and creamy substance (tomalley). Set aside. Remove lobster flesh and slice. Reserve.

✓ In a skillet, heat 1 tablespoon oil and 1 tablespoon butter. Sauté lobster for 5 minutes.

✓ To make the coulis, in a skillet, sauté onion in olive oil, add 3 chopped tomatoes, stir in balsamic vinegar.

✓ In a larger skillet for the main sauce, heat butter and oil, and sauté onion with ham and prosciutto. Add 2 diced tomatoes. Add coulis to sauce skillet, along with wine, garlic, and bouquet garni. Let wine evaporate. Stir in 1/2 cup brandy. Simmer 20 minutes.

✓ For the liaison, in a small saucepan, heat butter, sauté shallot until cleared. Remove pan from heat. Stir in mustard, mashed yolk, lemon juice, paprika, cayenne, pepper, and salt. Add to sauce, stirring until creamy.

✓ Pour brandy over sliced lobster. Ignite. Let flames subside. Coat with the "sauce à l'Américaine" and serve.

✓ Rice is a good accompaniment, or parsleyed potatoes.

✓ A Pouilly-Fuissé wine is recommended.

Serves 6

3 rock lobsters
1 bouquet garni
2 tablespoons butter
2 tablespoons olive oil
1/2 cup brandy

For the sauce:

1 tablespoon butter
1 tablespoon olive oil
1 large onion, finely chopped
2 ounces ham, finely chopped
2 ounces prosciutto, finely chopped
2 ripe tomatoes, peeled, seeded, and diced
1 cup white wine
1 bouquet garni
1/2 cup brandy

For the coulis:

1 onion, finely chopped
2 tablespoons olive oil
3 tomatoes, chopped
1 tablespoon balsamic vinegar

For the liaison:

1 tablespoon butter
1 shallot, finely chopped
3 garlic cloves, minced
1 tablespoon Dijon mustard
1 hard-boiled egg yolk, mashed
Juice of 1/2 lemon
1/2 teaspoon paprika
1/3 teaspoon cayenne
Pepper and salt

Monkfish in a Sauce of Normandy Apple Wine

Lotte au pommeau de Normandie

"The Pays d'Auge, my region of Normandy, happily combines the finest products of the sea and the land. Born on one of the oldest farms there, I grew up with this rich culinary culture."

Nicole Ameline
Deputy of Calvados

Pommeau is a wine made from apple must and eau-de-vie. Its strength could be compared to hard cider spiked with calvados, the apple brandy that takes its name from this department known for its orchards and dairy farms.

✔ In a skillet, heat butter, sauté monkfish 3 minutes on each side. Add shallots and apples and cook 5 more minutes. Pour in pommeau, ignite. Add cider. Cover and simmer 30 minutes over low heat. Stir in crème fraiche, reduce a few minutes. Season, sprinkle with chives, and serve.

Serves 4

4 tablespoons butter
4 filets monkfish
2 shallots, finely chopped
2 apples, cored and cubed
1/2 cup pommeau
1 cup hard cider
1 cup crème fraiche
Pepper and salt
3 tablespoons chives, finely chopped

Galette of Andouille Sausage on a Bed of Braised Leeks

Andouille de Vire sur fondue de poireaux

The north-facing beaches of Calvados in Lower Normandy were the scene of the D-day landings in 1944. Vire, the andouille capital, is in the department's hilly southern part. In America, andouilles are a specialty of New Orleans, an integral part of Cajun cuisine. Originally brought by the French to the New World, these smoked sausages have evolved into something entirely different. While the two are equally great specialties, Cajun andouilles are spicy and garlicky. The French ones are made of pork intestine and stomach—an entirely different process and taste.

In the town of Vire, where the French andouilles are most famous, the making of tripes is an artisanal tradition. After many washings, the innards are cut into strips, strung up, and smoked for three weeks. They are then immersed in water for a day, after which they are stuffed into the small intestine, encased in a net, and simmered for six hours. The finished sausage becomes gray. It is often served grilled. Andouilles are a permanent feature of French gastronomy.

"The andouilles from Vire are not merely internationally known and appreciated, they are also a large source of artisanal employment as well as great pride for the region."

Jean-Yves Cousin
Deputy of Calvados

Serves 4
1 pound leeks
4 tablespoons butter
1/4 pound slab bacon, cubed
1/2 pound French andouille
(can be mail-ordered from
D'Artagnan)
1 cup crème fraiche
4 tablespoons fond de veau
(veal stock)
Salt
Sprigs of chervil or other herb,
for garnish
For the galettes:
1/3 cup all-purpose flour
1/3 cup buckwheat flour
1 egg
1/2 cup water
Salt

✓ Combine galette ingredients with a little water to make a smooth batter. Let stand for 1 hour. In a skillet, make little galettes as you would when making pancakes. Set aside.

✓ Cut off green part of leeks and reserve for another use. Slit the whites vertically, wash free of sand, drain well, and dice finely. Sauté leeks gently in butter until they have given up their moisture.

✓ Meanwhile, cook the bacon cubes until golden. Drain and add to leeks.

✓ Stir in 2 tablespoons crème fraiche and adjust seasoning.

✓ In a nonstick pan about 7 inches in diameter, make 4 galettes.

✓ Cut andouille into 1/4-inch slices and warm in veal stock.

✓ To serve, spread each galette with a layer of leeks, add the andouille slices, top with remaining cream and a sprig or two of herbs.

Smashed Potatoes with Cheese and Lardons
Truffade

"The Cantal department in the Auvergne in south-central France is named after the Massif du Cantal, majestic but rather cold in winter because of its altitude. Herdsmen would take the cows into these mountains for several months each summer. They would live in burons, slate-roofed cabins of volcanic stone, and live off the Cantal resources, cheese and potatoes. Their high-pasture cow's milk has traditionally produced Appellation Contrôlée cheeses such as Salers and Cantal—rich, tangy, cheddar-style cheeses—while Bleu d'Auvergne, a soft and rich blue cheese, is made lower down. While the herdsmen were forbidden to cut into cheeses being aged, they could eat tomme fraîche, curds that had been pressed but not yet broken up and salted and molded.

"The name truffade comes from trufa or trufla, meaning potato in the Occitan patois of Auvergne. This traditional dish is prepared with Cantal cheese and potatoes. The herdsmen might eat it with sausages or slabs of boiled bacon. Other variations come with lardons or minced garlic."

Vincent Descoeur
Deputy of Cantal

✓ In a skillet, heat oil, sauté bacon and potatoes, cover and cook 15–20 minutes, stirring occasionally, until golden and crisp. Add cheese, crumbled. Toss and let melt. Add crème fraiche, garlic, and parsley. Check seasoning. When the whole mass comes together, the *truffade* is ready. Serve.

"There are several variations of truffade; I chose one I prefer. Truffade accompanies a well-marbled Salers steak perfectly, but is fully satisfying served by itself."

Serves 6
3 tablespoon olive oil
1/4 pound slab bacon, cubed
2 pounds potatoes, peeled and sliced
1 1/2 cups soft white cheese such as farmer's cheese
1/3 cup crème fraiche
3 garlic cloves, finely chopped
1/2 cup parsley, finely chopped
Pepper and a little salt

Snails in the Charente Manner

Cagouilles charentaises

All native chefs of small villages or provincial towns use escargots picked live in the fields and hedgerows after a rain, conditioned and prepared fresh. This of course does not apply to the way they are thought of, or prepared, in America. For authenticity's sake, here is the way escargots are cooked in the Charente. This recipe was provided by Martine Pinville, deputy of Charente.

✓ Over a large bowl topped with a sieve, mix snails with the kosher salt, vinegar, and flour. Leave for 2 hours to allow snails to purge themselves. Rinse under running water.

✓ In a large pot half full of water, put 1 tablespoon salt, peppercorns, carrots, parsley, thyme, bay leaf, 2 cloves garlic, and the onion. Bring to a boil, add snails. Reduce heat, and cook 1 hour. Drain, reserving liquid.

✓ Mince the shallots and 4 cloves garlic. In a pan, melt butter, sauté shallots, garlic, and remaining parsley. Cook 5 minutes until shallots are golden. Add pork sausage meat, broken up. Stir well, and cook 15 more minutes.

✓ Add snails, wine, and 1 cup reserved cooking liquid. Simmer 2 hours, stirring regularly, adding more liquid as needed. Adjust seasoning. Serve.

Serves 4

6 dozen small snails
1 1/2 cups kosher salt
1 tablespoon wine vinegar
1 tablespoon flour
1 tablespoon peppercorns
2 carrots, peeled and cut into thick pieces
Half bunch fresh parsley
4 sprigs thyme
1 bay leaf
6 garlic cloves, peeled
1 onion studded with 6 whole cloves
1/2 pound shallots
4 tablespoons butter
1/2 pound pork sausage meat
1/4 cup parsley, finely chopped
1 bottle ordinary red wine
Pepper and salt

Lamprey, Charente Style
Lamproie à la charentaise

The lamprey, an eel-shaped fish that inhabits coastal waters and rivers, is one of the oldest marine species. The flesh of the lamprey has a delicate flavor and is considered a luxury by gastronomes.

Often as long as one meter, the lamprey has no bones, no scales, and no jaws. A wide mouth with suckers enables the lamprey to attach itself to its prey, which it then nibbles. Fishing for lamprey demands dexterity. In both the Loire and Charente Rivers, it is a source of fishermen's pride. And this preparation of lamprey, a very old tradition in the Charente, is famous throughout France.

"Easy to prepare, this is a wonderfully savory dish. Serve the lamprey simply with grilled slices of bread.

"Be sure to accompany the dish with a local red wine from the Charente. Try one from Christophe Veral's Domaine les Folies."

Marie-Line Reynaud
Deputy of Charente

Serves 6

1 lamprey, about 3–4 pounds
Flour for dusting
3 tablespoons olive oil
2/3 cup pineau des Charentes (see note)
3–4 leeks, washed, trimmed, and cut up in 2-inch pieces
5 shallots, minced
2 1/2 cups red wine, preferably Charente
4 sugar cubes
6 prunes
1–2 pieces dark chocolate
1 bouquet garni (thyme, parsley, bay leaf)
Pepper and salt
2 tablespoons wine vinegar

✓ Similar to the method of cooking lobster, the lamprey is immersed in salted, boiling water. Cook 1 minute, no more. Remove from water. Hang the lamprey by its head. With a sharp knife, cut an incision near its tail to let its blood drain into a bowl. Then scrape the skin with a grater or a knife.

✓ Cut the fish in 2-inch pieces. Flour them and brown them in 2 tablespoons oil in a skillet. Pour in the pineau des Charentes and flambé. Reserve.

✓ In a heavy saucepan, sauté the leek sections and the shallots in 1 tablespoon oil. Add the wine and, when it boils, the sugar, prunes, chocolate, and bouquet garni. Season to taste. Simmer for 2 hours.

✓ Add the pieces of fish and simmer for 1/2 hour more. To thicken the sauce, stir in the blood mixed with the vinegar.

✓ Serve in bowls, with toast alongside.

Note: Pineau des Charentes is a fortified wine made from grape must and cognac. On the sweet side, and deliciously aromatic, it is often served as an aperitif. It is widely available in France and abroad.

Mussels in a Curry Sauce
Mouclade au curry

"I always find that removing one out of every two mussels from its shell makes the eating easier. A must: a finger bowl with a wedge of lemon for each guest!"

Jean-Claude Beaulieu
Deputy of Charente-Maritime

✓ Scrub each mussel under running water and remove the "beard."

✓ In a large kettle, cook mussels, wine, onion, pepper and salt, covered, shaking pot every 2–3 minutes to ensure even distribution of heat. After about 5 minutes, when all mussels are opened (a few may not), remove from heat. Place cheesecloth in a colander over a bowl, and strain. Reserve liquid, letting it cool, but keep mussels warm, covered.

✓ In a pan, sauté shallots in butter, stir in flour, and cook into a pale roux. Add reserved liquid, a little at a time, to form a light sauce. Add cream, curry, and pepper, and heat through.

✓ At serving time, place the egg yolk in a bowl. Pour in a little of the hot cream sauce, stirring steadily with a wooden spoon, and then gradually work in the rest of the sauce. (Do not return sauce to heat after combining with egg yolk, or it will "turn.")

✓ Pour the sauce over the warm mussels, toss well, and serve directly.

Serves 4

3 pounds mussels
1 bottle dry white wine
1 onion, finely chopped
3 shallots, finely chopped
3 tablespoons butter
1 tablespoon flour
1/2 cup heavy cream
1 tablespoon curry powder
Pepper
1 egg yolk

Mussels from La Rochelle
Mouclade rochelaise

"Mussels consumed in the area of La Rochelle come from the Bay of Aiguillon—a fertile spot for especially savory mussels. After the baby bivalves, or spat, are gathered as the tide permits, they are placed in nets on the famous **bouchots,** *stakes planted in mud flats where the mussels grow to full size and flavor."*

Maxime Bono
Deputy of Charente-Maritime

Serves 4

6 pounds mussels
4 tablespoons butter
1/2 cup heavy cream
1 cup dry white wine
2 egg yolks
1/4 cup cognac
1 bouquet garni (parsley, thyme, chives, bay leaf)
1/2 teaspoon saffron
2 onions, finely chopped
Pepper

✓ Clean mussels by scraping shells with a small knife, removing barnacles and beard, and scrub under running water.

✓ In a large pot, bring wine to a boil, add bouquet garni and mussels. Cover and cook 3–5 minutes, shaking pot to distribute heat, until all mussels are open. Turn heat off. Filter the broth through a colander lined with cheesecloth, and reserve. Remove mussels to an ovenproof dish, keeping the mussels on the half shell and discarding the empty tops.

✓ Preheat oven to 400°F.

✓ In a saucepan, melt butter, sauté onion until golden, stir broth in gradually, simmer 15 minutes. Add pepper and saffron.

✓ In a bowl, combine cream, egg yolks, and cognac. Add this to the saucepan of broth, stir well, and pour over mussels. Place the dish of mussels in the oven until heated through. Serve.

Champagne Oysters
Huîtres au champagne

The department of Charente-Maritime, where the Charente River flows into the Atlantic halfway up the west coast of France, is prime country for oysters. They may be savored at the source on the Île d'Oléron, or on the Île de Ré or overlooking the charming enclosed harbor of La Rochelle. "Warm oysters are extraordinary. All their flavor is concentrated, offering an iodine explosion to the palate. "One can enjoy this recipe as hors d'oeuvre with aperitifs, or as a first course with, of course, champagne."

Didier Quentin
Deputy of Charente-Maritime

Serves 4
24 oysters, preferably in the shell, or in a container with their liquor
3 egg yolks
1 cup crème fraiche
Juice of 1/2 lemon
1 tablespoon dill, finely chopped
1 cup champagne
Pepper
2 tablespoons butter
3 shallots, finely chopped

✓ Place a sieve on top of a bowl and shuck oysters over it, catching the liquor. Set aside oyster meat and half shells. If using already shucked oysters, separate liquor from meat.

✓ To the bowl of oyster liquor, add egg yolks, crème fraiche, lemon juice, dill, 1/2 cup champagne, and a grinding of pepper. Mix well.

✓ In a skillet, heat 1 tablespoon butter and sauté shallots until golden. Stir in the remaining 1/2 cup champagne and more pepper. Cook over low heat until most of the champagne has evaporated. Pour cream mixture in and cook down by half, stirring and watching that it does not boil. Add oysters to sauce and cook 2 minutes. Remove oysters and replace in their shells. Add remaining 1 tablespoon butter to sauce and whisk vigorously. Spoon sauce over oysters in their shells.

✓ Place oysters under broiler for 1 minute. Serve with toast points.

Mamelie's Bread Pudding

Gâteau de pain de Mamelie

This department, situated at the very center of France, takes its name from its main waterway, the River Cher. Sancerre, at the northeast edge beside the Loire, is known throughout the world for its excellent white wine. Because of its abundance of clay, a very active pottery culture has flourished in Sancerre as well.

"My grandmother wasn't rich, lived in a village, and as was often the case, she lived close to the poverty line. Imagination led to survival. Each day, I remember her creating dishes and desserts, generally delicious, out of practically nothing. It gives me pleasure to invite you to taste her special bread pudding."

Yves Fromion
Deputy of Cher

✓ Preheat oven to 350°F.

✓ In a bowl, mix bread cubes with milk. Add eggs, 1/2 cup sugar, and vanilla. Mix in sliced apples, raisins, and lemon zest. (For the zest you may substitute a liqueur or a spice such as cinnamon.)

✓ In a saucepan, stir 1/2 cup sugar with 1/2 cup water over medium heat until it becomes a blond caramel.

✓ Butter a mold such as a deep-dish pie plate. Pour caramel into mold, tilting to spread all over. Add apple mixture. Bake 30–45 minutes, or until a knife inserted in the center comes out clean. Let cool 10 minutes. Invert a serving plate over the pudding and flip to unmold. Serve warm or cold.

Serves 6

1 loaf stale French bread, cubed
2 cups milk
4 eggs, slightly beaten
1 cup sugar
1 tablespoon vanilla
4 apples, peeled, cored, and sliced
1 cup raisins
1 teaspoon zest of lemon

Potato Dumplings
Farcidure corrézienne

Named after the river Corrèze that rises in its mountains, the Corrèze department in the Limousin region is situated in south-central France. The ancient and rustic Corrèze specialty called farcidure—farce dure, hard stuffing—is a sort of potato dumpling. A mixture of raw, grated potatoes and potato purée is rolled into balls that are poached in simmering water until they rise to the surface, indicating they are cooked.
"While the Limousin cuisine suffers from an unflattering reputation for being austere, Corrèze chefs aspire to transform simple fare into attractive dishes, giving wings to ordinary ingredients. Farcidure is a perfect example."

Jean-Pierre Dupont
Deputy of Corrèze

Serves 6
1 pound salt pork, in a slab
3 cups chicken stock
8–10 pounds potatoes, grated
1 cup buckwheat flour
4 garlic cloves, minced
1/2 cup sorrel leaves, finely chopped
1 1/2 cups flat parsley, finely chopped
Pepper and salt
18 cubes bacon
18 cabbage leaves (optional)

✓ In a large kettle, cook salt pork with stock over low heat for 50–60 minutes, turning over regularly.

✓ Squeeze grated potatoes in a towel, extracting as much liquid as possible. In a large bowl, mix squeezed potato, buckwheat flour, garlic, sorrel, 1 cup parsley, pepper, and salt. With your hands, form egg-sized balls, incorporating a cube of bacon in each. Pack firmly, then flatten slightly to make patties. (If you like, you can wrap each patty in a cabbage leaf and tie with kitchen twine to avoid its breaking up.)

✓ Put patties in kettle with salt pork. Simmer, covered, until they rise to the surface, about 1 hour. Drain. Sprinkle with remaining parsley and serve with slices of the salt pork.

Potato Galettes with Swiss Chard and Leek

Farcidure grillée du pays d'Égletons (Milhassou)

"The famous farcidure is known to all Corréziens. But there are many towns in the Corrèze, each with its own farcidure, so to tell them apart, almost all of them bear a second name as well. Argentat's farcidure is called poule sans os or poule seize or colombette. The one from Brive is mique; from Treignac, mounassou. Only the dish from Tulle is referred to simply as farcidure. The one I offer here is called milhassou, picart, or chien d'Égletons.

"How could every Corrézien possibly cook the same way, after all, when one lives half a mile high and another almost at sea level? Some live on the banks of the Dordogne, near Quercy, some on the Millevaches Plateau. So many different altitudes, climates, cultures, within one department. Our cuisine reflects these differences.

"The milhassou has for its base potatoes. In the environs of Égletons, before the potato arrived, millet was the main fare. In those days people used to soak their millet, and because millet is rather bland, they added chopped herbs and vegetables. The farcidure was cooked in a bit of pork fat until crisp on one side, then on the other, et voilà!

"Then potatoes arrived. In order to give the potato a texture similar to that of millet, the women of the Corrèze devised a metal tool with points that scraped the potato into shreds. This tool has evolved into what we know today as a grater.

"This is how women fed their families, for years and years. On practically nothing. And yet the dish survived. Today, Corréziens salivate at the mere mention of farcidure.

"This farcidure recipe was given to me by my friend Régine Rossi Lagorce, author of several regional cookbooks."

François Hollande
Deputy of Corrèze

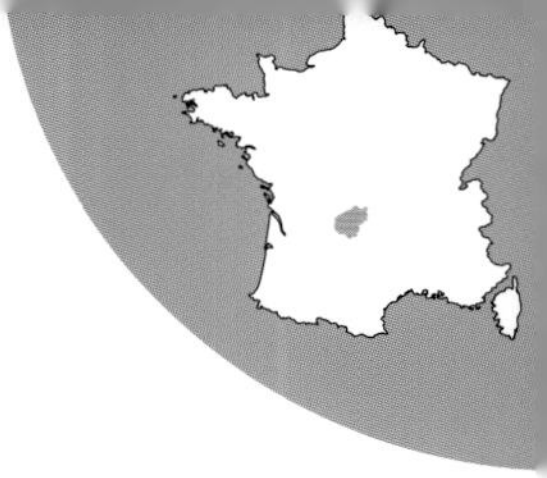

Potato Galettes with Swiss Chard and Leek

✓ To make the *farci*, grind leek, Swiss chard, onion, garlic, and parsley in the food processor, or chop finely by hand. Reserve.

✓ Change to the processor blade for julienning-grating. Grate potatoes. If you do not have a food processor, a simple grater will do fine.

✓ In a bowl, combine leek mixture with grated potatoes, salt, and pepper.

✓ In a pan, cook half the bacon cubes until they give up some of their fat. Add farcidure mixture, pressing down into a flat cake. Reduce heat and cook 10 minutes. Raise heat again briefly, so the bottom becomes brown and crisp. Reverse the galette onto a plate, cooked side up.

✓ Put the rest of the bacon into the pan and, when it has rendered a bit, slide the galette back into the pan and repeat the operation. When the second side is crisp and the center tender, serve.

This farcidure-milhassou can be the centerpiece of a meal, accompanied by a salad. It is also delicious served as a side dish with any kind of meat, roasted or in a sauce.

Serves 4

2 pounds Yukon gold potatoes
1/2 teaspoon salt
Pepper
1 cup slab bacon, cubed

For the *farci*:
1 leek, white only
3 small Swiss chard leaves
1 small onion
2 cloves garlic
2 parsley sprigs

19 CORRÈZE

Stuffed Eggplant
Aubergines farcies à la bonifacienne

Corsica is situated west of Italy and southeast of France. Naturally, given its proximity to the two countries, the island shows strong influences of both France and Italy in every aspect of its culture.

Once independent, Corsica was conquered by the French in 1769 and became part of metropolitan France in 1770. Napoléon Bonaparte, a native of Ajaccio on Corsica's west coast, was thus an infant when he became a citizen of the country he would rule.

In 1975 Corsica was divided into two departments, Haute-Corse and Corse-du-Sud.

"A perfect summer recipe, ideal for large buffet parties, these eggplants may be prepared in advance and are equally delicious served cold or hot."

Camille de Rocca Serra
Deputy of Corse-du-Sud (South Corsica)

Serves 12

12 medium-size eggplants, cut lengthwise
8 ounces fresh bread crumbs soaked in milk, squeezed dry
6 garlic cloves, minced
1/2 cup basil leaves, chopped
Pepper and salt
4 eggs
2 tablespoons butter, softened
1/2 cup grated Parmesan
Olive oil for frying

✓ Blanch the eggplant halves in boiling water or, better, steam them. Remove while still firm, let cool, and scoop out eggplant flesh. Press to remove as much liquid as possible.

✓ In a bowl, mix bread, eggplant, garlic, basil, pepper, and salt. Add the eggs one by one, then the butter and cheese. Stuff mixture into shell halves.

✓ In a wide pan, heat oil and fry each eggplant half, beginning with the stuffed side down. Drain. Serve alone or, if you wish, with a tomato sauce.

Quenelles of Swiss Chard and Cheese

Storzapreti

Corsicans consider brocciu, a soft, fresh whey cheese made from ewe's or goat's milk, their "national" food. Unlike Italian ricotta, brocciu is lactose-free.

"The literal translation of our Corsican storzapreti—*which is similar to the Italian pasta* strozzapreti *in name only—is strangle-the-priest! My choice of this recipe, it goes without saying, is neither religious nor political. It is purely gastronomic."*

Paul Giacobbi
Deputy of Haute-Corse (Upper Corsica)

✔ In a kettle of salted water, blanch Swiss chard leaves 3 minutes. Skim out and drain thoroughly. On a cutting board, chop Swiss chard and mint. In a bowl, mix the ricotta, egg, 1/4 cup Parmesan, pepper, and salt. Add Swiss chard and mint. Toss well.

✔ Flour a work surface and your hands. With 2 spoons, form quenelles. Roll them in the flour.

✔ In the same kettle, bring salted water to a boil. Drop the quenelles in, one by one, so they do not touch. After they rise to the surface, cook 5 minutes more. Drain.

✔ Pour tomato sauce into an ovenproof dish. Put storzapreti in dish and coat gently. Sprinkle with remaining 1/4 cup Parmesan cheese and bake 8 minutes until gratinéed. Serve.

✔ Good by itself or as an accompaniment.

Serves 4

2 bunches Swiss chard, or spinach, leaves removed from stems, washed
1/4 cup mint leaves or marjoram
1 pound ricotta or, if available, brocciu
1 egg
1/2 cup grated Parmesan cheese
Flour for dusting
Pepper and salt
1 cup prepared tomato sauce

Oysters Stuffed and Baked in Lettuce with Tomato Coulis
Petits tian d'huîtres Nustrale

A tian is an ovenproof earthenware dish originating in Provence. The gratin is baked in a tin or oven-proof casserole.
"This recipe, developed by Vincent Tabarani, president of Cucina Corsa, subtly combines traditional Corsican products of the land and the sea, showcasing the Nustrale oysters farmed in the Étang de Diane, an inlet near Aléria on Corsica's east coast. These oysters, famous for their nutlike flavor and their tenderness in the mouth, are only improved by being paired with brocciu, the creamy sheep or goat cheese that Corsicans call their 'national cheese.'"

Sauveur Gandolfi-Scheit
Deputy of Haute-Corse (Upper Corsica)

Serves 6
18 oysters
Kosher salt
1/2 cup white wine
Pepper
1 tablespoon olive oil
1/2 small onion, finely chopped
2 tomatoes, peeled and chopped
1 tablespoon balsamic vinegar
18 romaine leaves
1 cup ricotta cheese, drained
1/2 cup creamy goat cheese
1 egg, beaten
1 tablespoon parsley, finely chopped
1/4 cup parsley, cut into fine strips
2 ounces hard goat cheese, grated

✓ Open the oysters over a bowl, catching their liquor. Scrub the bottom half shells, dry them, and place them on a bed of kosher salt in a *tian* or other baking dish.
✓ Filter oyster liquor into a saucepan. Add white wine and a little pepper. Bring to a boil. Turn heat off. Immerse oysters for 4 seconds. Drain. Reserve
✓ In a skillet, make your coulis. Heat olive oil, add chopped onion and sauté until golden, add tomato, stir in balsamic vinegar and sauté 5 minutes. Reserve.
✓ In a kettle of boiling salted water, blanch romaine leaves for 2 seconds. Drain.
✓ In a small bowl, mix drained ricotta and soft goat cheese (or brocciu alone, if available) with egg and parsley. Spread the 18 salad leaves on a towel. Divide cheese mixture into 18 little mounds on the leaves. Place one oyster on each mound. Close the leaf around it, like a package.
✓ Pour a few drops of coulis into the bottom of each shell. Place an oyster package in each shell, seam side down, and sprinkle with grated goat cheese. Broil 2 minutes. Serve immediately, accompanied by a white Patrimoniu or a light red wine, well chilled.

Snails in a Mustard Sauce
Escargots à la moutarde

The Côte d'Or is a limestone escarpment of Burgundy that lends its name to the department. The east-facing slope of the Côte d'Or is home to some of the greatest wines of Burgundy.
Marc is a colorless brandy made from the distillation of grape skins. "This recipe with its famous escargots, its unctuous Dijon mustard, and its legendary marc de Bourgogne, is one of Burgundian cuisine's signature dishes."

Rémi Delatte
Deputy of Côte-d'Or

Serves 6
6 dozen snails, canned
4 tablespoons butter
1/2 cup marc or, if unavailable, vodka
2 cups crème fraiche
4 tablespoons Dijon mustard
Pepper and salt

✓ Rinse and drain snails. In a skillet, melt butter, sauté snails 5 minutes. Pour 1 tablespoon marc in and ignite. Stir until flames subside. Reserve snails and discard remaining butter.

✓ In the same skillet, stir crème fraiche, mustard, and remaining marc. Reduce by half. Season to taste. Stir the snails into the sauce. Serve hot in individual bowls with a crisp, warm baguette.

Coq au Vin from Burgundy

Coq au pinot de Bourgogne

"A noble product of high quality, chicken prepared in a pinot noir of Burgundy is mouthwatering. Offering gustatory satisfaction to a tableful of friends, coq au vin is one of the great classics of Burgundian cuisine. Its cooking is slow and long. Long enough for the sauce to be fully impregnated with its multiple flavors. When the aroma escaping from the Dutch oven reaches one, it is irresistible."

Bernard Depierre
Deputy of Côte-d'Or

✓ In a wide heavy-bottomed pot or Dutch oven, brown chicken in oil on all sides. Remove and reserve. In the same oil, sauté onion 5 minutes. Add carrots. Stir. Return chicken to pot with garlic, bouquet garni, pepper, and salt. Pour in cognac and ignite. Pour in wine. Stir and cover. Simmer over very low heat for at least 2 hours.

✓ In a skillet, sauté bacon and mushrooms. Stir into chicken. Remove bouquet garni and adjust seasoning.

✓ Sprinkle coq au vin with parsley, and serve with flat noodles or steamed potatoes.

Serves 8

1 large chicken, about 5–6 pounds, cut up
3 tablespoons olive oil
2 onions, minced
3 carrots, peeled and sliced
3 garlic cloves, crushed
1 bouquet garni (bay leaf, parsley, thyme)
Pepper and salt
1 cup cognac
1 bottle Burgundy pinot noir
1/2 pound slab bacon, cubed
8 ounces white mushrooms, diced
1 cup parsley, finely chopped

69

Eggs Poached in a Burgundy Wine Reduction

Oeufs en meurette

"People call our sumptuous Burgundy region a gastronomic paradise. Burgundy wines do tend to add depth and a unique dimension to our specialties.

"The following recipe, stemming from our home cooking tradition, may at first appear somewhat simple, but it requires a touch, a je-ne-sais-quoi to make it delicious."

François Sauvadet
Deputy of Côte-d'Or

Serves 4

1 tablespoon olive oil
2 shallots, minced
1 onion, diced
2 garlic cloves, 1 minced, 1 halved
1/4 pound bacon cubes (lardons)
1 bouquet garni (thyme, bay leaf, parsley, oregano)
1 bottle good Burgundy
Pepper and salt
1 heaping tablespoon flour
4–5 tablespoons butter
8 slices French baguette, or challah
8 eggs

✓ In a large skillet, heat oil. Over low heat, sauté shallots, onion, minced garlic, and bacon pieces. Pour in wine and add bouquet garni. Stirring occasionally, reduce liquid by half. Season. Strain into a bowl. Discard solids and return wine reduction to cleaned skillet. (This may be done to advantage the night before. Bring back to a simmer when ready to proceed.)

✓ With your fingers, blend flour into softened butter to make a beurre manié. Add to skillet. Stir well until sauce is smooth and thickened. Keep it hot but not boiling.

✓ Rub bread slices with cut garlic clove and toast them. Butter them lightly. Place 2 slices on each of 4 plates.

✓ In a strainer over a bowl, pour contents of skillet. Return strained sauce to skillet. One at a time, break eggs into a saucer and slide into sauce to poach. With a large spoon, move eggs gently so they stay separate and do not stick to bottom. After 3 minutes, lift each poached egg along with some sauce onto a toast. Serve.

Burgundy Fish Soup
Pochouse

"The pochouse is in a way the bouillabaisse of Burgundy. Unlike the bouillabaisse of Marseilles, made from sea fish, pochouse features freshwater fish, especially our rivers' famous perch. This traditional recipe introduces a Burgundy less familiar but, with its white wine sauce, Burgundian none the less."

Alain Suguenot
Deputy of Côte-d'Or

<u>Serves 10</u>
6–7 pounds freshwater fish, whole
2 leeks, washed and trimmed
3 carrots, peeled
5 garlic cloves, 4 minced, 1 halved
4 shallots, minced
1 bouquet garni (thyme, parsley, bay leaf)
Pepper and salt
2 bottles dry white Burgundy wine, preferably Aligoté
1/2 cup marc, or vodka
3 tablespoons butter
2 tablespoons flour
1/4 pound cubed bacon (lardons)
10 slices country-style bread

✓ Gut the fish. Cut off and reserve the heads and tails. Cut the bodies into 2-inch slices.

✓ In a large pot, put the fish heads and tails, leeks, carrots, minced garlic and shallots, bouquet garni, pepper, and salt. Pour in the white wine. Bring to a boil, reduce heat, cover, and simmer 30 minutes.

✓ Uncover and continue cooking until liquid has diminished by half.

✓ With your fingers, blend butter and flour into a beurre manié.

✓ Strain fish stock through a sieve into another pot. Discard solids. Incorporate beurre manié into stock, stirring until smooth. Bring back to a boil, flambé with marc, then add lardons and fish pieces. Cook 10 minutes.

✓ Toast or grill bread slices and rub with cut garlic.

✓ Check seasoning of soup. Serve accompanied by the garlic croutons.

Gateau of Crepes with a Lemon Cream

Gâteau de crêpes au citron "Nathalie"

The Côtes-d'Armor department, called Côtes-du-Nord until 1990, is situated in the north of Brittany.
"Both my grandmothers wore the traditional Breton costume that went down to their ankles, with the coiffe, the white headdress. Crepes are also deeply a part of traditional Breton cuisine, and always had a part in our family gatherings. Passed down from generation to generation, this crepe recipe has been modernized by my wife Nathalie."

Marc Le Fur
Deputy of Côtes-d'Armor

CREPES

✓ In a bowl, mix flour, salt, and sugar. Make a well in the center, drop egg yolks in, and mix. Gradually add milk, stirring until smooth. In a dry bowl, whip egg whites until stiff. Gently fold into flour mixture.

✓ In a crepe pan or regular frying pan, over medium heat, melt 1/4 teaspoon butter and pour in a small ladle of crepe batter. Swirl to distribute the batter evenly. Cook 2 minutes until bottom of crepe becomes golden. With a spatula, flip crepe over and cook a few more seconds. Reserve on a holding plate. Repeat until all crepes are cooked.

LEMON FILLING

✓ Zest 1 lemon. Put zest into a sieve. Plunge sieve into boiling water for 2 minutes. Remove and run cold water over zest. In a bowl, beat yolks with sugar and zest until mixture becomes creamy. Incorporate mascarpone and juice of 1 lemon. Beat until smooth and fluffy. Stir in coffee and rum.

ASSEMBLING THE CAKE

✓ For a neat appearance, ideally assemble the gateau in a cake mold of roughly the same diameter as the crepes.

✓ Alternate one crepe, lemon filling, ladyfingers to cover. Repeat until all is used, ending with a layer of lemon filling.

✓ In a small bowl mix juice of remaining lemon with lemon marmalade, and pour over cake.

✓ Cover with plastic wrap and refrigerate.

Serves 8

For the crepes:
3 1/2 cups unbleached flour
3/4 cup sugar
1/2 teaspoon salt
3 eggs, separated
4 cups milk
Butter for greasing pan

For the lemon filling:
2 lemons
6 egg yolks
2/3 cup sugar
1 pound mascarpone
1/2 cup strong black coffee
2 tablespoons rum
1/2 pound ladyfingers
3 tablespoons lemon marmalade

Hazelnut Cake
Gâteau creusois

"According to legend, the recipe for this delicious pastry came from a fifteenth-century parchment found among the fallen stones and rubble of a monastery in the area of Crocq, in the Creuse—one of the 83 departments created during the Revolution, when so many monasteries were destroyed. The monks cooked this creusois cake in ceramic tiles that were themselves creuses—hollow, concave, or curved . . .

"Meltingly soft and tender, it is said that each morsel of the gâteau creusois reveals the beauty, savory delight, and charm of its place of origin: La Creuse, in the heart of France."

Jean Auclair
Deputy of Creuse

✓ Preheat oven to 325°F. Spray or oil an 8-inch cake pan and dust with flour.

✓ In a medium bowl, or the container of your food processor, sift together 1/4 cup flour, 1/2 cup confectioners' sugar and salt. Add butter. Pulse 5 times. Add hazelnuts.

✓ In a dry bowl, whisk egg whites until they form soft peaks: do not overbeat. Combine egg whites gently with dry ingredients.

✓ Pour mixture into prepared cake pan, and bake 18–20 minutes. Remove from oven. Cool at least 10 minutes. Transfer to rack to finish cooling. Sift some confectioners' sugar over top of cake. Slice and serve.

Serves 6

1/4 cup unbleached flour
1/2 cup confectioner's sugar
Pinch of salt
1/3 cup hazelnuts, finely ground
4 egg whites
3 tablespoons butter, melted and cooled

Duck Pot-au-Feu and Cabbage Leaves Stuffed with Foie Gras

Pot-au-feu de canard et sa feuille de chou farcie au foie gras

The Dordogne department is in southwestern France, in Aquitaine, just east of the Bordeaux wine country. Its capital is Périgueux and most of its area was historically called the Périgord. Hilly and verdant, with many castles, the Dordogne is famous for its foie gras, duck, and gastronomy.

"Pot-au-feu, one of France's national dishes that originated on farms, is traditionally made from beef and vegetables. It should be prepared the day before, so the flavors have a chance to deepen and meld. Refrigerated overnight, its fat solidifies and is easily lifted off, leaving a clear broth. After reheating, the marrow from the beef bones is extracted and spread on warm brioche, served along with the broth.

"This typical Périgord pot-au-feu is prepared with duck meat, cooked with vegetables in a broth, and enhanced by slices of fresh foie gras nestled in cabbage leaves—a true delicacy!

"With this delectable local specialty, I recommend a local wine of the Domme country—a small collective of vintners with barely fifty acres revived in the last fifteen years, the Vignerons des Coteaux du Céou, at Florimont-Gaumier."

Germinal Peiro
Deputy of Dordogne

Serves 4

3 magrets (breast filets) of duck
4 duck thighs
4 duck gizzards
1 duck neck skin
Sea salt
4 bread slices, soaked in water and squeezed dry
1/2 pound pork sausage meat
2 eggs
Pepper and salt
12 cups chicken stock
1 onion, peeled and quartered
1 pound carrots, peeled and cut in chunks
4 leeks, white part only, well washed
1/2 pound turnips, peeled and quartered
2 celery stalks, cut in chunks
10–12 good-sized Savoy cabbage leaves
1 1/2 pounds fresh foie gras
1/4 teaspoon freshly grated nutmeg

✓ In a bowl, salt duck pieces liberally. Reserve. In another bowl, mix bread, sausage meat, eggs, pepper, and salt. Stuff mixture inside neck skin. Sew extremities with kitchen twine.

✓ Rinse salt off duck. In a large kettle, heat stock and simmer duck and stuffed neck for 1 hour. Add onion, carrots, leeks, turnips, celery. Continue cooking 30 minutes.

✓ In another kettle, boil water and blanch cabbage leaves 3 minutes. Drain on paper towel. Place a piece of foie gras in the center of each leaf. Sprinkle with nutmeg, pepper, and salt. Fold into a package and tie with kitchen twine.

✓ Shortly before serving, taste broth and adjust seasoning. Immerse cabbage packages and cook 5 minutes.

✓ With a slotted spoon, remove everything to a large platter. Slice the duck breasts and stuffed neck, and remove strings from cabbage. Moisten with a little broth. Serve.

Morteau Sausage with Smoked Pork and Haricots Verts

Une recette toute simple avec la saucisse de Morteau

"It's simple, it's healthy—this sausage from Morteau happens to be the leanest of all pork sausages—and it's delicious!"

Jean-Marie Binetruy
Deputy of Doubs

The sausage from the Morteau region, traditional and smoked, is famous throughout France.

Serves 4

1 Morteau sausage (see note)
1-pound slab bacon, uncut
3–4 potatoes, peeled and quartered
2 pounds extra-fine green beans (haricots verts)
Few sprigs parsley, finely chopped
Pepper and salt

✓ In a large pot, place sausage, bacon slab, potatoes, and water to cover. Bring to a boil, reduce heat, and cook 20 minutes. Add beans and continue cooking 8 minutes.

✓ Slice bacon and sausage, place on a platter, and surround with the beans and potatoes. Sprinkle with parsley, pepper, and a little salt. Serve.

Note: The authentic smoked sausage must come from Morteau in the Doubs, but a version made by a California charcutier can be ordered online at www.saveurdujour.com.

Montbéliard Sausage and Potatoes in Sauce
Pépéfier

The Montbéliard sausage, firm and delicately smoked like the Morteau, is smaller at six inches long. The Montbéliardais claim that it also is leaner.
"A traditional dish from the Montbéliard region, for those appreciating tastes of bygone days, the pépéfier can still be found today in many rural corners around Besançon. And it never fails to enchant."

Marcel Bonnot
Deputy of Doubs

✓ Peel, slice, and cook potatoes 15 minutes. Drain.
✓ In a pot, cover sausages with water, bring to a boil, reduce heat, and cook 25 minutes. Remove and slice sausages. Reserve cooking water.
✓ In a saucepan, heat olive oil, add flour, and allow to cook in, stirring. Slowly incorporate cooking water from sausage to form a creamy sauce. Season to taste, then add vinegar. Combine with potato and sausage. Serve.

Serves 4
2 Montbeliard sausages
3 pounds potatoes
1 tablespoon olive oil
2 tablespoons flour
2 tablespoons wine vinegar
Pepper and salt

Creamed Morels on Toast
Croûte aux morilles

"The first time I was served a croûte aux morilles *was on a June Sunday at the Auberge Marle in Myon, a tiny village tucked in a valley in the middle of nowhere, on the border between the Jura and Doubs departments. The dining room seemed filled and lively. When the man who would become my husband asked whether we could sit down and order lunch, the answer came quickly: Of course—if you don't mind sharing the menu being served for a christening lunch. We were only too pleased to accept.*
"The croûte aux morilles—*glory of the Franche-Comté's gastronomy— is featured in celebratory feasts, and remains for me a gustatory memory that reflects the incomparable aroma of the morel, king of mushrooms."*

Françoise Branget
Deputy of Doubs

<u>Serves 6</u>
1/4 pound dried morels
6 tablespoons butter
3 tablespoons flour
1 cup heavy cream
Pepper and salt
6 slices of bread

✓ In a bowl of hot water, immerse morels. After 2 hours, remove morels, filter the liquid, and reserve. Wash mushrooms under running water to remove any sand.
✓ In a saucepan, melt 3 tablespoons butter and stir in flour to make a light roux. Add morels and a ladle of mushroom liquid, continuing to stir, adding more mushroom liquid until it forms a smooth sauce. Simmer 20 minutes. Stir in heavy cream. Season to taste. Allow to reduce again for several minutes.
✓ In a frying pan, over low heat, melt 3 tablespoons butter and fry bread slices on both sides.
✓ Spoon the morel mixture evenly over the fried bread slices. Serve hot, with a white wine. As my district runs down to the Jura, I suggest the wines of M. Henri Colin from Le Moutherot or of M. Marcellin Puget from Buffard.

As a slight variation, to salute my Italian origins, I substitute polenta for the fried bread. I spread hot polenta thinly on a cookie sheet. When it has set, I cut it into rectangles, fry them in butter, and top with the creamed morels.

Lamb's Feet and Stomach Parcels, Crest Style

Défarde crestoise

The défarde *is a specialty of the town of Crest, situated in the Drôme, a mostly mountainous department just north of the Vaucluse, between the Rhône River and the Alps. The* défarde *is a close cousin of the* pieds et paquets *from Sisteron on page 14. This recipe was provided by Hervé Mariton, deputy of Drôme.*

Serves 4

4 pounds lamb tripes and stomachs
10 lamb's feet
1/2 cup cognac
2 pounds onions, peeled
2 pounds carrots, peeled
4 tomatoes, quartered
18 garlic cloves
2 cloves
1 large bouquet garni (parsley, celery with leaves, leek top, bay leaf, thyme)
1 bottle white wine
3 quarts chicken stock
Pepper and salt
4 tablespoons butter
4 tablespoons flour
1 bunch parsley
Juice of 1 lemon

✓ Wash tripes and stomachs in several waters. Cut stomachs into 2-inch squares. Fold them into parcels, using tripes to tie them up.

✓ Blanch stomach parcels and lamb's feet, refresh in cold water, and flambé with cognac. Check that feet are clean and free of hair.

✓ In the bottom of a large stockpot, place a plate upside down. Put in lamb's feet and parcels, whole onions and carrots, tomatoes, 12 peeled garlic cloves, 2 garlic cloves each stuck with 1 clove, and the bouquet garni. Add the bottle of wine and enough stock to cover. If necessary, make up the amount with water and bouillon cubes. Season lightly. Bring to a boil, lower heat, and simmer covered for 5 hours.

✓ Over another pot, place a large colander and pour everything into it. Remove the solids in the colander to a work area. Set the liquid back on the stove and reduce by half.

✓ Meanwhile, in a smaller casserole, place the lamb parcels. Pick all the bones out of the feet and add the deboned meat to the casserole.

✓ Press the cooked onions and garlic cloves through a fine sieve and add the puree thus obtained to the reduced cooking liquid.

✓ In a saucepan, melt butter, stir in flour, and cook until roux is nicely browned. Chop together parsley and remaining 4 garlic cloves to make a *persillade*. Add to roux. Moisten with lemon juice. Adjust seasoning.

✓ Pour sauce into casserole with lamb parcels and simmer for 1 hour more. Serve hot.

Apricot Tart with Montélimar Nougat

Tarte à l'abricot et au nougat de Montélimar

Montélimar, on the east bank of the Rhône, is the second largest town in the Drôme, after Valence. The city is known for its nougat, a confection made of sugar paste and toasted nuts. You can see stands selling artisanal nougat in every outdoor market in the South of France. Nougat can be purchased in America in candy shops.

"Montélimar nougat is famous beyond our frontiers. Sold throughout the world, it is made with natural local ingredients. For generations nougat has evoked the image of a Provence Gourmande. Apricots, the pride of the Drôme, combine with our sugary delicacy in this dessert to offer an authentic, inimitable flavor of Provence."

Franck Reynier
Deputy of Drôme

✓ In the food processor, grind pistachios finely. In a wide bowl, sift them together with flour, salt, and confectioners' sugar. Mix in butter with your fingers, then 1 egg and vanilla. Knead, working the dough with the heel of your hand. When smooth, gather into a ball, cover with plastic wrap, and chill for 30 minutes.

✓ Roll out dough. Place in a tart mold lined with parchment paper. Trim and crimp edges of dough. Prick all over with a fork. Return to refrigerator.

✓ Preheat oven to 350°F.

✓ In a bowl, beat 2 eggs with sugar until pale. Add cream and almond extract. Set aside. Bake the empty pie shell for 10 minutes. (To keep it flat in "blind" baking, a temporary filling of pie weights or dried beans on a layer of parchment paper may be used.)

✓ In the prebaked shell, place a layer of apricot halves. Sprinkle with nougat bits. Pour cream mixture in and tilt to distribute evenly.

✓ Bake for 10 minutes, remove briefly to decorate with a few pistachios, and return to oven for a final 10 minutes.

Serves 8

For the *pâte sablée*:
30 unsalted pistachios, finely ground
1 1/2 cups flour
1 tablespoon confectioners' sugar
1 teaspoon vanilla extract
1/2 teaspoon salt
8 tablespoons butter, softened
1 egg

For the filling and finishing:
2 eggs
1/4 cup sugar
3/4 cup heavy cream
3 drops almond extract
2 cups canned apricots
1 cup nougat, broken into pieces
Chopped pistachios for garnish

Stuffed Turkey Escalopes in Cider and Cream

Paupiettes au cidre

The Eure department, in Upper Normandy, takes its name from the river Eure, though the Seine also passes through. Like all of Normandy, the Eure is cider country.

Paupiettes are thin slices of meat rolled around a stuffing and served in a sauce of choice. Today one may find them fully prepared in French charcuteries. Paupiettes are made with either beef, veal ("veal birds"), chicken, or turkey, as well as fish. I have chosen here a paupiette recipe with turkey escalopes. This recipe was provided by Marc Vampa, deputy of Eure.

Serves 6

1/2 pound white mushrooms, wiped and sliced
2 tablespoons butter
2 tablespoons olive oil
1 cup finely ground turkey
1 onion, minced
3 tablespoons breadcrumbs
1 egg
1/4 cup parsley, chopped finely
3 sage leaves, chopped finely
Pepper and salt
6 turkey escalopes
1/2 cup calvados
3 cups hard cider
1/2 cup heavy cream

✓ In a pan, heat 1 tablespoon each of butter and oil, sauté mushrooms 10 minutes. Set aside.

✓ In a bowl, combine ground turkey, onion, breadcrumbs, egg, parsley, sage, pepper, and salt. Mix well.

✓ Place each escalope between wax paper and pound until flatter and wider.

✓ Fill each escalope with one-sixth of the stuffing. Roll, and tie with kitchen twine.

✓ In a skillet, heat remaining butter and oil. Sauté paupiettes until nicely browned on all sides. Add calvados and flambé. Add contents of mushroom pan. Pour in cider, enough to come halfway up the paupiettes. Cover and simmer for 30 minutes.

✓ Stir in cream and let it warm up. Adjust seasoning. Serve.

Duck and Foie Gras Pâté from Chartres

Pâté de Chartres

Chartres, merely an hour from Paris, is one of France's most beautiful medieval towns, with one of the greatest cathedrals in the world. Chartres is also known for its gastronomy. The pâté de Chartres is its great specialty. In fact, the Chartres residents consider their pâté their second cultural monument.
"This recipe, given to me by Lionel Cousanon, chef of the Bistrot de la Cathédrale, has origins lost in the mists of time. Its composition has varied over the centuries with the presence of the birds hunted in the Beauce. The golden plover, favored in the Middle Ages, has practically disappeared. Wild duck, partridge, and pheasants are now all used as the hunting season progresses. But one thing does not change: the large chunks that stud this pâté."

Jean-Pierre Gorges
Deputy of Eure-et-Loir

✓ In a bowl, combine flour, butter, salt, egg yolk, water, to form a smooth dough. Let rest 15 minutes or more in the refrigerator.

✓ Sort the duck meat by quality. Take the best parts, particularly the breast, and cut them into *aiguillettes*, or spears. Set these aside.

✓ Mince the rest of the duck meat finely. Mix it in a bowl with pork, veal/turkey, egg, port wine, cognac, pepper, and salt.

✓ Remove dough from refrigerator, roll out two-thirds into a rectangle, and fit it into the bottom and sides of a loaf pan. Roll out remaining third of dough for a lid.

✓ Begin filling mold with meat mixture interspersed with *aiguillettes* of duck breast. Halfway up, insert foie gras slices in a single layer, then add rest of *aiguillettes* and meat mixture. Cover with remaining dough, pinching to seal properly. Let pâté rest overnight in the refrigerator before baking.

✓ Preheat oven to 325°F.

✓ Make a hole in the pastry lid and insert a funnel of aluminum foil to allow steam to escape. Bake 2 1/2 hours.

✓ Escape of steam will have left a hollow under the pastry lid. Prepare 2 cups gelatin. Pour slowly through funnel until space is filled. Allow to cool.

✓ Finally—and this is important—refrigerate for 3 days before serving.

Serves 15

For the crust:
1 1/2 cups flour
6 tablespoons clarified butter
1/2 teaspoon salt
1 egg yolk
1/4 cup cold water

For the filling:
1 duck, boned (about 2 pounds meat)
1 1/2 pounds pork, half coarsely ground, half finely ground
1/2 pound veal or turkey meat, half coarsely ground, half finely ground
1 egg
1/4 cup port wine
1/4 cup cognac
Pepper and salt
1 fresh foie gras lobe, sliced lengthwise
4 tablespoons gelatin, dissolved in 2 cups warm water, and 2 tablespoons Brandy. Let it cool and set aside.

Meat and Vegetable Soup with Boiled Bread Pudding

Kig ar farz de Plounévez-Lochrist

At the northwestern tip of France, in Brittany, the department of Finistère (Land's End) is well named. Bretons have their own language. This recipe—a kind of pot-au-feu made to fend off cold Brittany winters—consists of various meats (kig) and vegetables cooked slowly in a broth with a bread pudding (farz) made from either buckwheat (farz noir) or plain flour (farz blanc), or even one of each. Nourishing and hearty, it predates the arrival of potatoes in France.

"This regional recipe varies according to what particular part of Brittany it is made in. Here the farz, after it is cooked, is crumbled over the soup. In other Breton areas it is sliced like a sausage, and fried."

Jacques Le Guen
Deputy of Finistère

Serves 4

1 pound beef short ribs
1 pound pork hock
1/2 pound slab bacon
2 onions, peeled
4 carrots, peeled
2 leeks, well washed and cut into chunks
1 cabbage, quartered and blanched
Pepper and salt

For the farz:

1 1/2 cups flour
1 1/2 cups milk
4 tablespoons butter
1 egg
Salt
1 cup raisins

✓ In a large kettle, cover meats by several inches of water, add pepper and salt, and bring to a boil. Reduce heat and simmer for 1/2 hour.

✓ Meanwhile, in a bowl, mix flour, milk, butter, egg, and salt. If needed, add a little meat liquid to reach the consistency of a pancake batter. Add raisins. Pour batter into a canvas bag about 8 by 12 inches, and tie the top securely with kitchen twine. The bag should be only two-thirds full, to allow for expansion.

✓ Skim surface of broth, and put the filled bag in the kettle with broth and meat. Add onions, carrots, and leeks. Simmer 1 1/2 hours. Add cabbage, cooking 1 more hour.

✓ Remove *farz* bag, drain, and open. Serve broth with meats and vegetables. Crumble *farz* over each filled soup plate.

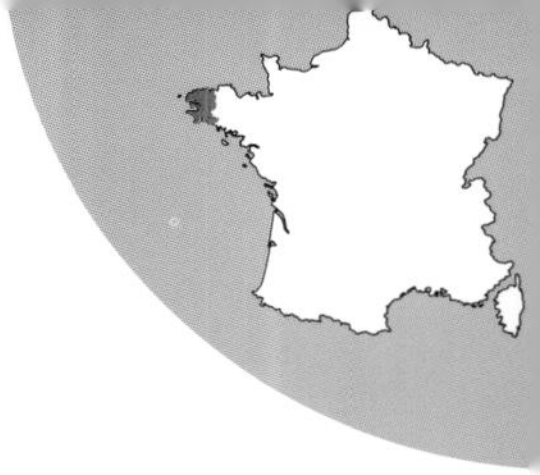

Breton Apple Cake
Far four

Far four, *from the Breton* farz fourn, *means "oven-baked." It originated in the eighteenth century with the* farz—*the savory accompaniment to the previous meat dish,* kig ar farz—*and through the years evolved into a flanlike dessert. It can be prepared with apples or raisins or prunes, or no fruit at all.*
"The far four, *a very old Breton recipe, evokes many childhood memories for me. This dessert, easy-to-prepare as well as affordable, belongs to Brittany's gastronomic patrimony."*

Marguerite Lamour
Deputy of Finistère

✓ Butter an ovenproof dish. Preheat oven to 400°F.
✓ In a bowl, break the eggs, whisk in sugar until pale, then add flour and milk. Pour batter into buttered dish. Place apple slices on top. Bake 15 minutes. Reduce heat to 300°F and continue baking for 30 minutes or until a knife inserted in the center comes out clean.
✓ Optional: Sprinkle with confectioners' sugar.
✓ Serve either warm or cold.

Serves 6
5 eggs
1/2 cup sugar
1 1/4 cups flour
3 cups milk
2 apples, peeled, cored, and sliced

Lobster, Breton Style

Homard à l'armoricaine

In Roman times, what is now Brittany was referred to as the Armorican Peninsula. Later, a Gaulish tribe lived on its northern coast. Historians and gastronomes have attached the name armoricain to Brittany ever since. Today a confusion between Armorican and American continues however, suggesting that those who call their dish "Homard à l'Américaine" really mean "à l'Armoricaine." Be that as it may, this lobster recipe is a typical Breton recipe, often prepared by my grandmother. It can also be made with crayfish. This recipe was provided by Christian Menard, deputy of Finistère.

Serves 6

3 lobsters
20 tablespoons salted butter
4 tablespoons peanut oil
Pinch of cayenne pepper
Pepper and salt
3 ounces cognac
1 bottle white wine, preferably Muscadet
5 shallots, minced
3 onions, minced
3 garlic cloves, minced
1 cup parsley, finely chopped
1 tablespoon tarragon
1/4 cup tomato paste

✓ Take the live lobsters, detach the heads and claws, and chop the bodies into 3–4 pieces. Reserve in a bowl all the liquid that comes out, and scoop the green matter into the bowl as well. [This process isn't for every cook. I suggest asking the fishmonger to execute it.—*Tr.*]

✓ In a large skillet over high heat, melt 10 tablespoons butter with the oil and sauté lobster pieces, turning with tongs until all pieces turn bright red—about 3 minutes on each side. Sprinkle with cayenne, pepper, and salt. Pour in the cognac and ignite. Let flames subside. Pour in the Muscadet.

✓ In another skillet, melt 7 tablespoons butter and sauté the shallots and onions, then stir in the garlic, parsley, tarragon, and tomato paste. Add onion mixture to lobster skillet, tossing well with a wooden spoon to distribute evenly. Cook 15 minutes, stirring regularly.

✓ With the tongs, remove lobster pieces to a serving platter and keep warm. Continue to cook the sauce briskly, reducing it by half.

✓ In a large saucepan, mash remaining 3 tablespoons butter with the reserved green matter and liquid from the raw lobsters. Place a sieve over the saucepan, and strain the contents of the skillet. Whisk well, then add the lobster pieces and rewarm for a few minutes. Serve.

Eggplant Caviar
Caviar d'aubergines

Located in southern France at the eastern limit of the Languedoc, and named after the river Gardon, the department of the Gard is best known for the Pont du Gard, the spectacular three-level arcaded Roman aqueduct-bridge dating back twenty centuries. The Gard also makes wines, most notably rosés to be served chilled with warm-weather meals.
"This delicious eggplant caviar can be eaten hot or cold, accompanied by a tomato-basil sauce."

William Dumas
Deputy of Gard

✓ Butter an ovenproof dish. Preheat oven to 450°F.
✓ Steam the eggplant until soft, 15 minutes. Mash with fork.
✓ In a bowl, whisk eggs, cream, pepper, and salt. Mix in mashed eggplant and chopped basil. Pour mixture into buttered dish.
✓ Bake 30 minutes. Serve.

Serves 8

6–7 eggplants, peeled and cubed
5 eggs
1/2 cup crème fraiche
Pepper and salt
1/2 cup fresh basil, finely chopped

Stuffed Squid

Encornets farcis à la Yvette Laïck

"Our cuisine of the South, bright colored, redolent of the Mediterranean, the sun, and olive oil, combined with the bounty of the sea, brings all these aromas together on our palates and our plates. I have chosen the delicious stuffed squid made by my grandmother."

Yvan Lachaud
Deputy of Gard

Serves 4

4 large squid
2 hard-boiled eggs
3 garlic cloves
1/2 cup parsley, finely chopped
1/2 cup mint, finely chopped
2 slices bread, soaked in milk and squeezed
1/4 teaspoon freshly grated nutmeg
Pepper and salt
1 raw egg
4 tablespoons olive oil
2 tablespoons cognac
1/2 green pepper, diced
1 onion, grated
1 shallot, finely chopped
1 bay leaf
2 sprigs thyme
1 tomato, peeled and diced
1 teaspoon tomato paste
1 tablespoon flour
1 bottle dry white wine

For the accompaniment:

1 cup rice
1 tablespoon butter
1 tablespoon crème fraiche
8 large shrimp
1 tablespoon cognac

✓ Clean squid under running water. Pat bodies dry. Reserve tentacles for the stuffing.

✓ Chop the tentacles and hard-boiled eggs. In a bowl, mix them with 1 minced garlic clove, half the parsley and mint, the soaked bread, nutmeg, pepper, and salt. Add the raw egg, mix well, and stuff squid bodies with mixture.

✓ In a deep skillet, heat 2 tablespoons olive oil, sauté stuffed squid until they turn light brown on all sides. Pour in cognac. Ignite and wait until flames subside. With tongs, remove squid and reserve.

✓ In same skillet, add 1 tablespoon oil if needed, sauté green pepper, then add grated onion, shallot, 1 crushed garlic clove, remaining mint, leaves from 1 sprig thyme, bay leaf, diced tomato, and tomato paste. Stir well and allow to cook down a bit.

✓ Blend sauce ingredients in a blender and return to skillet, or simply mash them. Add flour to thicken, and stir in white wine. Return squid to skillet. Cover and simmer for 1 hour.

✓ Prepare the accompanying rice. When cooked, add butter and crème fraiche, pepper and salt. Pack cooked rice into 4 ramequins.

✓ In a small skillet, heat 2 tablespoons olive oil and sauté shrimp, 1 minced garlic clove, and remaining parsley for about 3 minutes.

✓ Remove squid from skillet and cut into thick slices. On a serving platter, unmold rice ramequins, place shrimp on top of rice, and surround with sliced squid. Coat with sauce. Pour and ignite remaining cognac, and carry to table. It's a spectacular entrance.

Monkfish Stew from Le Grau-du-Roi

Bourride de lotte graulenne

Le Grau-du-Roi, a small, pretty resort town and fishing port on the Mediterranean, is the only village in the Gard department with a harbor.

"This dish, long considered plat de pauvres *or pauper's fare, is now proudly presented at weddings and christening banquets. But first, a bit of history.*

"During the Roman occupation, Provence—then called Provincia Romana—extended from Lake Geneva to Toulouse. This recipe came to us with the Foire de Beaucaire, the famous weeklong fair where, from the thirteenth to the nineteenth century, merchants from all the lands of the Mediterranean converged on Beaucaire to trade, and to celebrate a veritable Babel of gustatory influences. Food was everywhere; people could sample delicacies in the streets. One of the delicacies was this monkfish recipe. In 1805 the Canal du Midi was extended from Sète to Beaucaire, joining the Garonne River to the Rhône. Frédéric Mistral, Provençal poet and 1904 Nobel laureate, sang the praises of the Beaucaire Fair in his Poème du Rhône.*"*

Étienne Mourrut
Deputy of Gard

✔ Put strained fish stock in kettle and poach monkfish for 10 minutes. Meanwhile, start potatoes steaming or boiling in a separate pot. Slice day-old bread and put it in a basket.

✔ With a slotted spoon, remove monkfish to serving platter and keep warm, surrounding it with potatoes when they are done.

✔ In a saucepan, over low heat, whisk yolks with 3/4 cup aioli, and gradually pour in 1 cup fish broth, stirring constantly until the sauce is thick enough to coat a spoon. Make sure it doesn't boil. Remove from heat.

✔ Pour sauce over fish, and serve with potatoes and bread slices. Pass remaining aioli separately, to spread on the bread.

Serves 6
Fish stock (recipe below)
3 pounds monkfish
1 1/2 pounds small potatoes
3 egg yolks
1 1/2 cups aioli (page 3)
1 loaf day-old bread
Pepper and salt

FISH STOCK (*FUMET DE POISSON*)

1 1/2 pounds fish bones	1 fennel bulb, diced
3 tablespoons butter	1/2 cup white wine
1 onion, diced	1 bouquet garni (thyme, bay leaf, oregano, parsley)
1 shallot, minced	
1 carrot, diced	Pepper and salt, as needed

✔ Clean fish bones under running water. Drain. Crush bones.

✔ In a kettle, heat butter, sauté onion, shallot, carrot, and fennel 5 minutes. Add fish bones, stir for 3 minutes more. Add wine, bouquet garni, and enough water to barely cover. Bring to a boil, reduce heat to simmer, and cook 25 minutes. Skim surface every few minutes. Adjust seasoning. Pass through a sieve.

✔ Mash minced garlic with salt to make a paste. In a bowl, mix garlic paste with yolks, whisk a few minutes. Trickle oil in, and continue whisking until it forms a kind of mayonnaise. Add pepper to taste.

Chicken and Vegetables with Red Pesto

Galinette au pistou rouge

"Legend has it that in the fourteenth century when the papacy was in Avignon, Pope Urban V fell gravely ill. His doctor prescribed the broth of galinettes, a variety of hen that in medieval times was raised only in a town in the Gard, called Bagnols-sur-Cèze. The pope in desperation made the journey to drink the broth—and was restored. On his return to the Papal Palace, the crowds in Avignon shouted, 'Miracle!' and a grateful Urban V offered the town of Bagnols-sur-Cèze a purse of gold coins."

Jean-Marc Roubaud
Deputy of Gard

✓ The day before, make the broth. In a kettle, with the chicken, put carrot, onion studded with cloves, whole garlic cloves, bouquet garni, ginger, peppercorns, and sea salt. Cover generously with cold water, bring slowly to a boil, and simmer very gently for 3 hours, skimming during first 1/2 hour. Let chicken cool in broth. Refrigerate meat and broth separately.

✓ Make the red pesto. In the food processor, mix crushed garlic, raw pine nuts, basil, pepper, and salt. With the motor on, drizzle oil in to form a loose paste. Transfer to a bowl and mix in minced tomatoes.

✓ In a skillet, heat 2 tablespoons oil, sauté scallions a few minutes until lightly colored. Add zucchini, fava beans, green peas, asparagus, and just enough chicken broth to cover. Simmer, covered, stirring occasionally, until vegetables are tender and broth has become thick and a little syrupy.

✓ Slice cold chicken, place on serving platter, surround with warm vegetables, and sprinkle with toasted pine nuts and black olives. Serve red pesto alongside.

Serves 6

1 organic chicken, 4–5 pounds
1 carrot, peeled and quartered
1 small onion, peeled
2 cloves
2 garlic cloves
1 slice fresh ginger
1 bouquet garni (celery stalk, parsley, thyme, bay leaf)
1 teaspoon mixed peppercorns
2 teaspoons sea salt from Provence, or kosher salt
2 tablespoons olive oil
Bunch of scallions, cut into 1-inch lengths
6 small zucchini, quartered lengthwise
1/2 pound shelled fava beans, blanched and peeled
1/2 pound shelled green peas
24 green asparagus tips
3 tablespoons pine nuts, toasted
24 black olives, pitted

For the red pesto:

2 garlic cloves, peeled and crushed
3 tablespoons raw pine nuts
1 cup fresh basil
Pepper and salt
1/2 cup olive oil
1 pound tomatoes, peeled, seeded, and minced

Foie Gras in a Madeira Sauce

Escalopes de foie gras au madère

The Haute-Garonne department, bordering on Spain at the midpoint of the Pyrenees, is traversed by the upper reaches of the river Garonne, which generates hydroelectric power in the south and waters a fertile plain to the north. This recipe was provided by Gérard Bapt, deputy of Haute-Garonne.

Serves 6

4 tablespoons butter
1 small onion, finely chopped
1/2 cup light cream
1 cup Madeira wine
2 tablespoons cornstarch
Truffle oil
Freshly ground pepper and sea salt
1/3 cup port wine
8 ounces white mushrooms, sliced
1 fresh foie gras, deveined
6 slices challah bread, toasted
1 black truffle (optional)

✓ First make a Madeira sauce. In a saucepan, heat 2 tablespoons butter and sauté onion until cleared. Gradually whisk in cream and Madeira. In a cup, stir cornstarch with just enough water to dissolve it. Add to sauce and whisk until it thickens. Add truffle oil, pepper, and salt. Remove from heat, stir in port wine, and reserve.

✓ In a skillet, heat remaining 2 tablespoons butter. Sauté mushrooms until golden. Pepper liberally. Reserve.

✓ Cut foie gras into 6 slices. Salt and pepper each slice.

✓ Heat a skillet dry—without any fat—sauté foie gras 1 minute on each side, or just until it begins to contract and to release fat. Don't oversauté because most of it will melt into fat. The interior should remain creamy.

✓ Place each slice of foie gras on a slice of toasted challah, cover with mushrooms, and top with Madeira sauce. Sprinkle with thinly shaved truffle.

Filet of Lamb with Rosemary and Garlic

Canon d'agneau rôti au romarin et jus aillé

Situated in Gascony in southwest France, the Gers department sits just north of the Pyrenées.
"Combining the pleasures of being both diverse and uncomplicated, Gersoise gastronomy has an international reputation. Its better-known dishes, foie gras and duck confit, are particularly delicious with quality wines. This recipe for a canon, or boneless loin, of lamb comes from Bernard Ramouneda of the restaurant Le Florida-in Castéra-Verduzan, and represents well the simplicity of Southwest cuisine."

Gisèle Biemouret
Deputy of Gers

Serves 4

1–2 canons of lamb, about 2 pounds
Pepper and salt
2 tablespoons olive oil
3 garlic cloves
2 large sprigs rosemary, or 2 tablespoons dried

✓ Ask your butcher to bone out the meat that otherwise would have been cut into loin lamb chops, to obtain the filet called a canon.
✓ Preheat oven to 350°F.
✓ Rub pepper and salt on all sides of the lamb and place in a roasting pan. Lubricate with olive oil. Add garlic cloves and rosemary sprigs. If using dried rosemary, crush and sprinkle over meat.
✓ Roast 30–35 minutes. (To check for doneness, pinch meat. As soon as you encounter resistance, it's perfectly medium-rare.) Let rest 15 minutes, covered in tented foil. Carve into medallions and serve with the exuded cooking juices.

Gratin of White Asparagus
Gratin d'asperges du Blayais

In Aquitaine, southwestern France, the Gironde estuary, formed by the confluence of the river Garonne with the Dordogne, gives its name to the department, world-renowned as the producer of Bordeaux wines. "Asparagus from the Blaye area, cultivated in black sand where it acquires its famous white color and tenderness, is considered the best asparagus in France. This gratin showcases its exceptional qualities."

Philippe Plisson
Deputy of Gironde

✓ Clean, trim, and peel asparagus. Cut into 3-inch pieces.

✓ In a large skillet, heat 3 tablespoons butter and sauté asparagus. They are delicate, so stir carefully with a wooden utensil to avoid breaking them.

✓ Season lightly and add water to cover, along with lemon juice to retain whiteness. Cover and cook over low heat for about 20 minutes.

✓ Preheat oven to 400°F.

✓ Transfer asparagus to a large gratin dish, or 4 individual ones. Pour in heavy cream, dot with remaining butter, and sprinkle with grated cheese.

✓ Bake 10 minutes. Serve immediately.

Serves 4
2 pounds white asparagus
4 tablespoons butter
Pepper and salt
Juice of 1 lemon
1 cup heavy cream
1 cup grated cheese

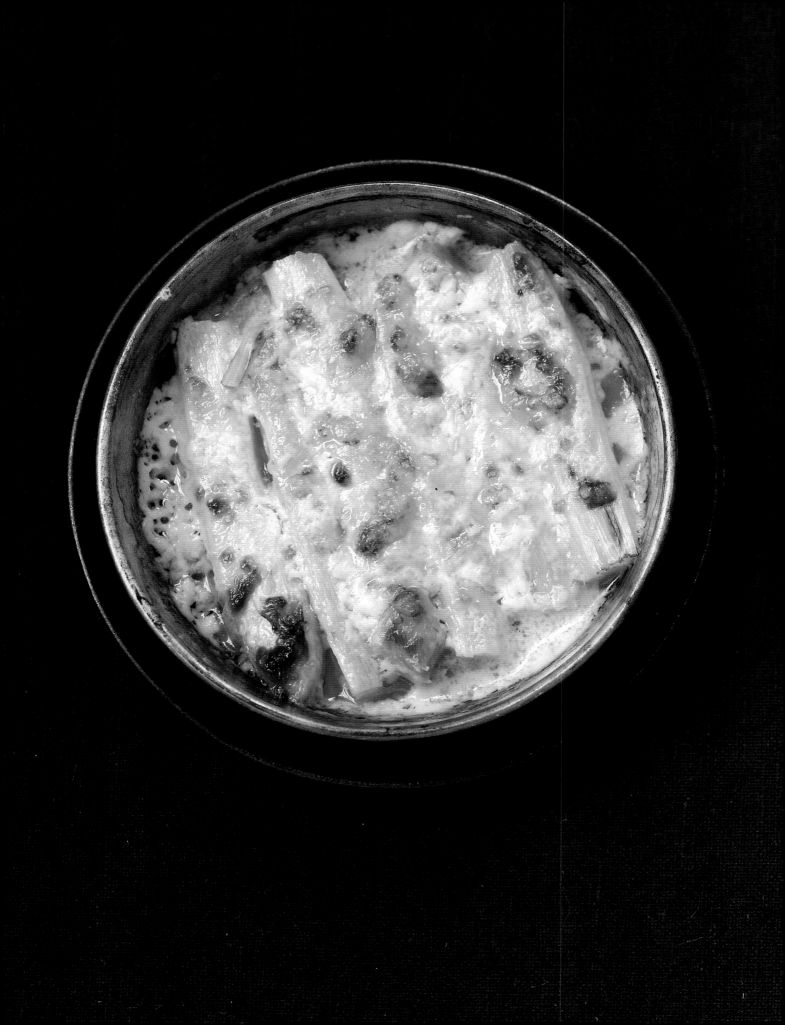

Stuffed Calamari
Calamars farcis

"The aroma of this easy-to-prepare and delectable Mediterranean dish summons images of southern France. The entire dish can be prepared ahead, the day before or in the morning, and refrigerated. It gains in flavor upon being reheated over low heat (not in the microwave). You may opt to serve it as a starter or as the main course. Delicious accompanied by a well-chilled white wine such as chardonnay."

Jean-Pierre Grand
Deputy of Hérault

Serves 4–6

8–12 calamari cleaned by the fishmonger
4 slices French bread, soaked in milk and squeezed dry
1 1/2 cups ground turkey, or lean sausage meat
1/2 cup parsley, chopped
2 garlic cloves, crushed
Pepper and salt
3 tablespoons olive oil
1 pound crushed tomatoes, fresh or canned
1 cup white wine
Pinch of saffron

✓ If your fishmonger has not done it, empty and clean calamari under running water and remove quills. Dry with paper towel. Reserve tentacles.

✓ In the food processor, combine soaked and squeezed bread, ground meat, parsley, garlic, pepper, and salt. Pulse to form a rough paste. Fill calamari with stuffing. Close each with a toothpick.

✓ In a skillet, heat olive oil and lightly brown calamari on all sides. Turn heat up, pour in wine, and cook 2–3 seconds. Reduce heat, cover, and simmer 30 minutes. Add chopped tentacles, tomato purée, and saffron. Season to taste. Continue simmering 20 minutes until sauce is smooth.

✓ Serve with rice.

Cuttlefish with Red Aioli
Rouille de seiche façon palavasienne

The Hérault, in the Languedoc region of southern France, extends from the Cévennes to the Mediterranean. Close to the departmental capital, Montpellier, the fishermen's village of Palavas-les-Flots lies on a strip of sand dunes that separates two saltwater lakes, the Étang de l'Arnel and the Étang du Méjean. Cuttlefish in a spicy mayonnaise sauce, called **rouille** *for its rust color, is a renowned specialty of the Montpellier area.*
"This recipe, developed through the expertise of the Brotherhood of the Rouille of Palavas-les-Flots, is my favorite. You can come and taste it during our Saint Peter's fair at Palavas in July."

Jacques Domergue
Deputy of Hérault

Serves 6

5 pounds cuttlefish
1/3 cup olive oil
3 onions, diced
6 ounces bacon cubes (lardons)
1 pound crabmeat
1/2 cup cognac
1/2 cup tomato paste
3 tomatoes, peeled
1 cup white wine
2 pounds potatoes, diced
1/4 teaspoon salt

For the rouille:

1 egg yolk
1/2 teaspoon sea salt
3 garlic cloves, finely minced
1/4 teaspoon hot paprika
1/4 teaspoon cayenne pepper
Juice of 1/2 lemon
1 cup olive oil

✓ For the rouille, put yolk and salt in the blender. Turn blender to high speed. Add garlic, paprika, cayenne, and lemon juice, and drizzle olive oil in until the sauce becomes firm. Refrigerate until serving time.

✓ Clean the cuttlefish, cut into chunks or rings, and blanch briefly. Set aside.

✓ In a skillet, heat olive oil and sauté onions and lardons until golden. Add crabmeat and stir. Pour in cognac and ignite. When flames subside, stir in tomato paste, whole tomatoes, white wine, potatoes, and salt. Simmer 45 minutes, uncovered. Add cuttlefish. Cook an additional 15 minutes. Stir in the rouille. Serve immediately.

Offcuts in a Pot (Pie) (Stewed Scraps, Soubès Style)
Entrée de Soubès

"The entrée, or first course, of Soubès—sometimes called a ragout of escoubilles, meaning 'scraps' or 'throwaways' in patois—takes its name from the charming twelfth-century hilltop village of Soubès, and is indeed made of simple ingredients. The dish is appreciated in the wider district of Lodève, fifty kilometers from Montpellier. In the course of time, home chefs in nearby Clermont-l'Hérault have elaborated on the dish, elevating its presentation from humble to more sophisticated by encasing it in puff pastry and calling it a croustade. In earlier days, when not everyone owned an oven, the dish was brought to the neighborhood baker, who added the crust and baked it.

"This regional specialty's local variants—from Soubès, Lodève, Clermont-l'Hérault, three lovely communes of the Hérault department—demonstrate once more the breadth of French creativity and ingenuity in turning leavings or leftovers into gourmet meals."

Robert Lecou
Deputy of Hérault

✓ Preheat oven to 350°F.

✓ In a heavy-bottomed pot, heat olive oil and sauté bacon, onions, garlic, and meats until nicely browned. Add carrots, celery, tomato, mushrooms, potatoes, tomato paste, chicken stock, thyme, and pepper and salt to taste. Stir to combine and simmer 1 hour. Rinse olives and stir in. Serve.

✓ This dish is better prepared ahead and reheated. You may opt to roll out some pastry dough (puff pastry or other) and encase the preparation. Brush with egg wash and bake 35 minutes before serving.

This dish is a distant cousin of the Cornish pasty and the American pot pie.

Serves 6

1/2 cup olive oil
6 ounces bacon cubes (lardons)
1 onion, chopped
3 garlic cloves, minced
3–4 pounds mixed meat scraps—chicken parts, pork, lamb, veal, beef, sausage
3 carrots, peeled and sliced
1 celery stalk, peeled and cubed
1 tomato, peeled, seeded, and chopped
1/3 cup dry porcini mushrooms, reconstituted in hot water
5 potatoes, peeled and cubed
3 tablespoons tomato paste
2 cups chicken stock
1 sprig thyme
Pepper and salt
1 cup pitted black or green olives

Broiled Lobster with Cream
Homard grillé sauce à la crème

Ille-et-Vilaine is the easternmost department of Brittany, where fishing is the main industry. Like Maine, where one can find the most delicious lobsters in the United States, Brittany prides itself on having the only lobsters worth the name in France. This recipe was provided by Marcel Rogemont, deputy of Ille-et-Vilaine.

Serves 2
1 lobster
2 tablespoons butter, melted
1/2 cup heavy cream
1/3 cup cognac
Pepper and salt
2 tablespoons tarragon

✓ In a kettle of briskly boiling water, cook lobster 12 minutes. Drain. With a sharp knife, cut lobster in half lengthwise. Collect all liquid from the inside of the lobster, as well as the creamy parts, green and pink, and roe if there is any.

✓ Turn broiler on high. Pour melted butter over halves, broil 10 minutes.

✓ In the meantime, in a saucepan, simmer and whisk cognac, cream, lobster liquid and creamy parts, pepper, and salt. When the lobster is cooked, add tarragon to sauce. Pour over broiled halves and serve immediately.

Mashed Potato and Cheese Pie

Marianne

"This traditional savory recipe from the town of La Châtre, in the Indre department in central France—George Sand country—is served either as an hors d'oeuvre with aperitifs or as a first course at the table."

Nicolas Forissier
Deputy of Indre

Serves 4

For the pâte brisée:
8 tablespoons butter
1 1/2 cups unbleached flour
1 egg
4 tablespoons ice water
1/2 teaspoon salt

For the filling:
1 pound Yukon gold potatoes, peeled and quartered
1 Epoisses cheese
1 tablespoon crème fraiche or sour cream
Pepper and salt
2 tablespoons butter

✓ In the food processor, combine all the pastry ingredients and pulse until a unified ball forms. Remove, cover with plastic wrap, and let rest in the refrigerator 30 minutes.

✓ Preheat oven to 350°F.

✓ Line a tart mold with the dough, prick with a fork, return to refrigerator. When oven is heated, prebake pie crust 10 minutes.

✓ Meanwhile, in a kettle, bring salted water to a boil. Cook potatoes 15–20 minutes. Drain. In a bowl, with a fork, mash potatoes with the cheese, crème fraiche, pepper, and salt.

✓ Fill prebaked pie crust with the mashed potato mixture. Dot with butter. Bake 35 minutes. Serve warm.

Pike in Beurre Blanc and Vouvray Sauce

Dos de sandre de Loire au beurre blanc, au vin de Vouvray

Situated in west-central France, the department of Indre-et-Loire boasts many of the most celebrated châteaux of the Loire valley—Chenonceaux, Amboise, Azay-le-Rideau—and celebrated wines as well. The sandre, pike perch in English and a near cousin to the American walleye, is a freshwater fish from the Loire. As aggressive a predator as the pike, it can be up to a meter long. This preparation of sandre is the pride of Loire cuisine.
"The Loire with its abundance of fish, the surrounding hills, the wealth of produce, all contribute to giving our territory a unique quality of life. I have chosen the following recipe, created by Didier Edon of Les Hautes Roches in Rochecorbon, for to me this recipe defines perfectly our Touraine gastronomy. As our native son François Rabelais wrote, 'L'appétit vient en mangeant, la soif s'en va en buvant' (The appetite increases with eating, thirst vanishes with drinking)."

Claude Greff
Deputy of Indre-et-Loire

✓ Prepare the fish portions (or have your fishmonger do it) by cutting it crosswise into 6 thick slices or, better, boning the fish to produce 6 nice filet sections.

✓ In a kettle, bring fish stock—1 shallot, garlic, carrot, celery, bouquet garni, and wine to a boil. Reduce heat, simmer 30 minutes. Set the fish stock aside.

✓ In a small bowl, whisk vinegar with salt and pepper, then with oil, to make a vinaigrette.

✓ In a skillet, melt butter, sauté remaining minced shallot until translucent. Season lightly. Reserve.

✓ Poach the oysters in fish stock for 30 seconds, refresh in cold water, and mash them. Set aside.

✓ Make the beurre blanc: In a saucepan, simmer the sliced shallots in the wine and vinegar until the liquid has all cooked off and the shallots are very soft. Whisk in the chilled butter, bit by bit. When the sauce is thick and smooth, add pepper and salt to taste. If it seems a bit too acidic, add a pinch of sugar as well. Keep the beurre blanc warm over simmering water until serving time.

✓ Place 6 plates in a warming oven.

✓ In a buttered fish poacher or kettle, put fish pieces, fish stock to cover, and lemon juice. Bring to a boil, immediately cover and remove from the heat, and leave to poach for 5–8 minutes, depending on the thickness of the pieces. With a slotted spoon, remove fish. Drain on a clean dish towel. Place each fish piece on a warmed plate. Coat with beurre blanc.

Serves 6

1 3-pound pike perch, scaled
1 quart fish stock—preferably freshly made, but can be purchased in markets or fishmongers
2 shallots, minced
1 garlic clove, minced
1 carrot, peeled and diced
1 stalk celery, diced
1 bouquet garni
1 cup dry Vouvray wine
1 tablespoon wine vinegar
Pepper and salt
3 tablespoons olive oil
2 tablespoons butter
6 oysters, shucked, oyster liquid reserved
Juice of one lemon

For the beurre blanc:
2 sticks cold butter, diced
4 shallots, finely sliced
3/4 cup dry Vouvray wine
1 cup white vinegar
Pepper and salt

Pike in Beurre Blanc and Vouvray Sauce

✓ Accompany the fish with an assortment of steamed small vegetables such as fingerling potatoes, baby carrots, extra-fine green beans (haricots verts), pearl onions, snow peas. Butter vegetables lightly and sprinkle with parsley. Place the vegetables around the fish in a ring. Serve.

Note: If the beurre blanc separates, do not panic. In a small saucepan, bring 1/4 cup heavy cream to a boil. Whisk in the broken sauce little by little, and it will reconstitute itself.

Foie Gras on Lacquered Pork with an Emulsion of Creamed Celeriac

Foie gras poêlé sur rillons laqués, emulsion de crème de céleri-rave

"This dish was produced on the occasion of an excellent dinner with a local restaurateur and local producers."

Michel Lezeau
Deputy of Indre-et-Loire

Serves 4

1/2 cup sugar
1 cup water
1 1/4 cups port wine
1/2 pound pork belly in one piece, rind removed
2/3 cup *fond brun* (can be purchased in specialty gourmet shops)
1/2 teaspoon herbes de Provence
1/2 celeriac, peeled and cubed
1 1/2 cup heavy cream
1/4 cup milk
1 lobe foie gras, cut into 4 generous escalopes
1/3 cup hazelnuts, toasted and chopped

✓ In a heavy-bottomed saucepan, over medium heat, melt sugar and cook 1–2 minutes or until it turns amber. Deglaze the caramel with a little port wine. Reserve.

✓ In a skillet, brown the pork belly on both sides. Deglaze with port wine, then add *fond brun* and herbes de Provence. Simmer, covered, for 4 hours.

✓ In a small saucepan, cook celeriac for 10 minutes in cream and milk. Purée in the blender, or mash and whip until smooth. Reserve.

✓ When pork is cooked, remove, and increase heat under sauce so that it reduces and becomes syrupy. Cut pork into thick slices—ideally 8—and turn them in the reduced sauce so that they become lacquered.

✓ Place 4 rimmed plates in a warming oven. Divide the pork slices between them.

✓ Heat a skillet without any fat. Flash sear foie gras escalopes 1 minute on each side.

✓ Place foie gras on top of pork, surround with celeriac emulsion, and sprinkle with caramel and chopped hazelnuts.

✓ Serve, accompanied by a mâche salad dressed in walnut oil.

Heirloom Organic Chicken from the Touraine

Géline de Touraine

The géline de Touraine, a chicken with dark plumage often referred to as dame noire, was historically raised only in the region around Tours. Known for its succulent meat, the géline is in great demand today by the chefs of fine restaurants throughout France.

"Thanks to INRA, our national agronomic research institute, and to dedicated organizations intent on preserving this nearly extinct breed of fowl, géline farming has resumed in Indre-et-Loire. In 2001 the géline was accorded the Red Label, the first heirloom breed to receive this distinction. I have chosen a recipe from the historic town of Loches because in its simplicity it perfectly demonstrates the subtlety of flavors of Touraine gastronomy while preserving the delicate tenderness of our Black Lady."

Marisol Touraine
Deputy of Indre-et-Loire

✔ Cut the chicken into serving pieces.

✔ In a skillet, heat butter. Brown chicken on all sides. Add onion and mushrooms. Reduce heat, cover, and cook 1 hour.

✔ Stir in 1 glass wine, and cook a few more minutes. Remove chicken pieces and reduce liquid while stirring in crème fraiche to make a smooth sauce. Return chicken to sauce. Season to taste.

✔ Serve with the rest of the bottle of Vouvray.

Serves 4

1 5-pound chicken, preferably organic

4 tablespoons butter

1 onion, chopped

1 pound mushrooms (shitaki or cremini or, if possible, chanterelles), sliced

1 glass white wine (Vouvray)

1/2 cup crème fraiche

Pepper and salt

Meat and Mushroom Pie
Tourte muroise

The department of Isère takes its name from the river that flows through Grenoble, gateway to the French Alps.
"This recipe is well known to the natives of La Mure, a very old mining town in south Isère. I vividly remember a lady of the town telling me how, when she was a little girl, her grandmother used to bake this meat pie in their coal stove for her husband, who would take it in his carryall for his meals down in the mine. Today, the coal mines are closed. There is, however, an underground museum, La Mine Image, commemorating those miners who came not only from La Mure but from all over the world, seeking a better life."

Didier Migaud
Deputy of Isère

Serves 5–6
1 pound veal (or turkey) meat, diced
10 ounces pork, diced
Pastry dough (pâte brisée) for a two-crust pie
1 cup green olives, pitted, well rinsed
4 ounces mushrooms (chanterelles, cremini, shitaki), chopped
1 egg yolk, lightly beaten with 2 tablespoon water (egg wash)

For the marinade:
1/3 cup olive oil
3 cups white wine
1 1/2 cups Madeira, or cognac if preferred
3 garlic cloves, sliced
1 onion, sliced
1 sprig thyme
1 bay leaf
1 cup parsley, finely chopped
1/2 cup chervil, finely chopped
1/2 teaspoon freshly ground nutmeg
1 clove
Pepper and salt

✓ Combine all marinade ingredients. Mix in both meats. Put in plastic bag and refrigerate overnight. The meat should absorb the marinade.

✓ Preheat oven to 325°F.

✓ To use as a *tourtière*, choose a deep-dish pie plate or a rectangular baking dish. Divide pastry dough unevenly. Roll out larger part and fit into bottom of *tourtière*, letting dough overhang.

✓ Remove meat from refrigerator. Discard bay leaf, thyme, clove, and a portion of the sliced onions and garlic. Take meat from marinade and place in *tourtière*. Add green olives, mushrooms, and enough marinade to moisten the filling. Roll out remaining pastry and place on top of pie. Seal the pastry tightly all around. Cut out a small hole in the middle of top pastry. Insert a cylinder of aluminum foil or parchment paper to act as chimney, allowing steam to escape. Brush top with egg wash. Draw a design on the pastry with the back of a fork. Bake 1 hour.

✓ May be enjoyed hot or cold. A green salad is a good accompaniment.

Potato Gratin
Gratin dauphinois

"The gratin dauphinois is a traditional recipe from the Dauphiné, the province that became the post-Revolution departments of Isère, Drôme, and Hautes-Alpes. (Indeed, it was demands by the Dauphiné in 1788 that precipitated the end of the ancien régime.) This dish, emblematic of our territory, is easy to prepare and delicious to enjoy with family and friends."

André Vallini
Deputy of Isère

"This recipe was given to me by a cousin who for decades has delighted gourmands in north Isère. It accompanies any meat well."

Alain Moyne-Bressand
Deputy of Isère

✓ Preheat oven to 350°F
✓ Rub garlic in an ovenproof dish, butter it, and coat the bottom with crème fraiche. Add a layer of potatoes, then a layer of crème fraiche sprinkled with garlic, nutmeg, pepper, and salt. Continue alternating layers, ending with crème fraiche.
✓ Bake 1 hour, or until the potatoes are tender and the top is crisp and golden. Serve.

Serves 4

2 pounds potatoes, peeled and thinly sliced
2 cups crème fraiche
2 garlic cloves, minced
1/4 teaspoon grated nutmeg
Pepper and salt

Snails Vienne Style
Escargots à la viennoise

Confusingly, the name Vienne applies in French to the capital of Austria, and to a river and a department in west-central France, as well as to the city in the Isère that sits on the left bank of the Rhône River, south of Lyon. Celebrated in history, this city was also made a gastronomic center in the early twentieth century by the legendary chef Fernand Point.

"May our friends in Burgundy forgive us for claiming their specialty and making it ours. I would remind them that Vienne was, in the fourteenth century, the capital of Provence, and before that was capital of the ancient kingdom of Burgundy. And the man who became Pope Calixtus II came from Vienne and was none other than Guy of Burgundy.

"What makes our stuffing different? The nuts add to the flavor of the terroir. The breadcrumbs give consistency to the melted butter. And the restrained use of garlic makes our escargots easy to digest."

Jacques Remiller
Deputy of Isère

Serves 6
6 dozen snails
2 carrots, sliced
1 onion, studded with 4 cloves
1 bay leaf
1 sprig thyme
6 hazelnuts, or 10 pistachios, skin removed
3 sticks butter, softened
3 garlic cloves, minced
1 slice sandwich bread, crumbled finely
2 tablespoons pastis
1 bunch parsley, finely chopped
Pepper and salt

✓ The picking of snails, after a storm, must by law be done after the first of July, and the snails must be at least 1 1/4 inches in diameter, with a limit of six dozen snails per person.

✓ Place snails in an airy cage and let them fast for 10 days or, if the weather is too hot, 6–7 days, watering them now and then. The night before preparing them, water them to make them come out of their shells, and sprinkle with 1–2 cups kosher salt. In the morning, rinse them with water and vinegar. Repeat salting and rinsing with vinegar water at least eight times.

✓ In a large kettle, bring water—without salt—to a boil. Cook snails 2 minutes. Drain and let cool. With a knife, remove snails from shells, trim. Wash snails again several times in water and vinegar, making sure all the slime is gone. Drain again.

✓ In a kettle half filled with water, place carrots, onion, bay leaf, and thyme. Bring to a boil and simmer snails 2 hours.

✓ Meanwhile, wash shells in vinegar and water. Drain.

✓ Finely grind the nuts. Combine with the butter, garlic, bread, pastis, parsley, pepper, and salt. Mix thoroughly with a fork.

✓ In each shell, insert a little butter, then one snail, and fill rest of shell with butter mixture. Place prepared snails in an ovenproof dish, open ends up, so butter will not run out. Bake 10 minutes, until butter bubbles.

✓ Serve with warm French baguette.

[This was how it was prepared then (and still is, in Burgundy). Today, however, especially in cities, picking and purging snails has become obsolete. I recommend buying snails already cleaned and cooked, in cans. Proceed directly to preparing the butter filling and stuffing the shells. Bake and serve.—Tr.]

Trout with Vin Jaune Sauce
Truite au vin jaune

The department of Jura in eastern France is home to the extraordinary and famous vin jaune *or yellow wine. Unique to this region, and produced by every one of the Jura châteaux, it is made from late-harvested Savagnin grapes. The wine is aged in oak barrels under a* voile *or veil of yeast for a minimum of six years before bottling, which imparts its walnut flavor and yellow color.*

"Our Jura wine, pure and characteristic, imparts its full flavor particularly well when used to prepare trout from our high Jura Mountain rivers. Potato purée combined with our local comté cheese is an ideal accompaniment to this delicious trout recipe."

Marie-Christine Dalloz
Deputy of Jura

✓ Heat a warming oven.

✓ Sprinkle the trout on both sides with pepper and salt. In a large skillet, melt 3 tablespoons butter over low heat and cook trout until crisp outside and tender inside, about 5 minutes on each side. Remove trout to a platter and keep warm.

✓ In the same skillet, heat remaining tablespoon butter and sauté shallot until golden. Reduce heat, pour in wine, stirring well to deglaze the pan, and simmer for 5 minutes. Add cream, continue stirring until thickened, and adjust seasoning.

✓ Return trout to sauce, and serve.

Serves 6

6 trout, cleaned and whole
Pepper and salt
4 tablespoons butter
1 cup crème fraiche
1 small shallot, finely chopped
1 cup yellow wine

Chicken Slivers in Comté Cheese and White Wine Sauce "Val d'Amour"

Émincé de poulet et sa sauce au comté et au vin blanc, façon Val d'Amour

"Easy to prepare, inexpensive, and perfect to enjoy among friends and family, this recipe shows to advantage the products of our Jura.
"The Jura department is prime AOC territory, awarded the sought-after label guaranteeing place of origin and authenticity for products ranging from our famous vin jaune *to our fruity cheeses—Comté, Morbier, bleu de Gex—and not forgetting the premium poultry, charcuterie, and escargots that have inspired our chefs. The chicken dish named for the Val d'Amour region is a perfect example of Jura's gastronomic creativity."*

Jean-Marie Sermier
Deputy of Jura

Serves 4

2 tablespoons butter
4 chicken breasts, thinly sliced
1 1/2 cups light cream
1 1/3 cups grated Comté cheese, or Cheddar
Pepper and salt
1/3 cup white wine

✓ Place 4 plates in a warming oven.
✓ In a skillet, heat butter and sauté chicken 10–15 minutes, until light brown and tender.
✓ Meanwhile, in a saucepan, heat cream with cheese, stirring until thickened. Add pepper and salt to taste.
✓ When chicken is done, remove to plates and keep warm. Stir wine into skillet to deglaze, then stir into cream and cheese.
✓ Spoon sauce over chicken. Serve with rice or noodles or, for something less usual, potato pancakes—and with the rest of the bottle of wine used in the deglazing.

Cake from the Landes Country

Pastis landais

The Landes department, on the southern part of France's Atlantic coast, is one of the country's largest departments—and the flattest. At the turn of the nineteenth century it was mostly landes *(heath or moorland), hence its name. Later, foresighted people began planting pine trees to stabilize the dunes and installing drainage, and the landscape changed. This recipe was prepared by Jean-Pierre Dufau, deputy of Landes.*

✓ In a small bowl, dilute yeast with a few grains of sugar and 3 tablespoons warm water. Leave it to "proof" for 5 minutes.

✓ Melt 9 tablespoons of the butter. In a large bowl, mix the flour, sugar, and salt, and make a well in the middle. Pour in melted butter, egg yolks, vanilla, and rum. Mix well. Stir in yeast.

✓ Whip egg whites until firm. With a rubber spatula, fold them into the flour mixture. Let dough rise about 1 hour, until doubled in size.

✓ Preheat oven to 450°F.

✓ With the remaining butter, grease a cake pan large enough that it is only half filled when you add the dough. Bake about 45 minutes, or until a knife inserted in the center comes out clean.

"Serve with a custard sauce. The pastis landais, our regional pastry, can also be made with prunes, or with orange flower water or anisette."

Serves 6

2 tablespoons dry yeast
10 tablespoons butter
3 cups flour
2/3 cup sugar
Pinch of salt
3 eggs, separated
1 tablespoon vanilla extract
2 tablespoons rum

Pistachio Macaroons with a Raspberry Coulis
Macarons pistache framboise

In north-central France at the heart of the Loire valley is the department of Loir-et-Cher, named after the river Loir (no -e) in the more fertile northern half and the river Cher in the marshy south. Between the two runs the mighty Loire (into which both Loir and Cher empty, farther downstream), drawing visitors to explore the local châteaux—Chambord, Chaumont, Cheverny, Blois—and the local cuisine. This recipe was provided by Nicolas Perruchot, deputy of Loir-et-Cher.

For the pistachio ganache:
1 cup pistachios, ground
1 1/2 cups sugar
2 egg whites
2 1/3 cups heavy cream
12 ounces white chocolate, chopped
3 1/2 sticks unsalted butter, softened
1/4 cup cornstarch

For the macaroons:
2 cups egg whites
1/4 cup water
1 1/4 cups granulated sugar
2 cups confectioners' sugar
1/2 pound almond flour
2 drops green food coloring

For the coulis:
2 cups raspberries
1/2 cup sugar

✓ Make the pistachio ganache: In the food processor, grind pistachios, 1/2 cup sugar, and egg whites into a thick paste. In a saucepan, bring 2 cups cream to a boil together with 1 cup sugar and pistachio paste. Let cool. Stir in remaining 1/3 cup cream mixed with cornstarch. Heat, stirring, until it thickens. Mix in white chocolate. Let cool to body temperature, then stir in soft butter gently, being careful not to incorporate air. Reserve.

✓ Make the coulis: In the blender, purée raspberries. In a saucepan, heat purée with the sugar until sugar is dissolved. Reserve.

✓ For the macaroons, beat the egg whites until firm. Place half in a separate small bowl.

✓ Dissolve the granulated sugar in the water, heating it to about 240°F (soft ball stage on a candy thermometer). Slowly drizzle sugar syrup over half the beaten egg whites.

✓ In a large bowl, mix together confectioners' sugar, almond flour, remaining egg whites, and green coloring. With a spatula, fold in warm meringue with confectioners' mixture and stir to reduce. It should be smooth and shiny.

✓ Line a baking sheet with parchment paper. Drop spoonfuls of macaroon paste, 1 inch apart, on parchment paper. (If you have a pastry bag, use a 1/2-inch nozzle.) Allow macaroons to rest on sheet for 30 minutes.

✓ Preheat oven to 300°F. Bake 15 minutes. Cool.

✓ Spread ganache over a macaroon, cover with second macaroon to form a sandwich, and press lightly.

✓ Serve pistachio macaroons with the raspberry coulis.

✓ Macaroons are better the second day.

Puff Pastry with Blue Cheese and Pear

Feuilleté à la fourme et poire

The river from which the Loire department in east-central France takes its name is the country's longest, at more than one thousand kilometers. The Loire valley is often called "the garden of France" for its flowers, vineyards, rolling hills.
The blue-veined Fourme de Montbrison and its cousin Fourme d'Ambert are among France's oldest cheeses, dating back to Roman times. The Latin casei forma, cheese mold, gave modern languages the words Käse, queso, and "cheese" along with formaggio and fromage—and the original forma was the tall cylinder still used for Fourme de Montbrison. Made with cow's milk, it is lightly fermented and remains soft.
"With our feet planted on our native earth, our head looking up at the stars above the Forez, our palate wrapped in the velvety, rich flavors of our region, life couldn't be better here!"

Jean-François Chossy
Deputy of Loire

✓ Peel, halve, and core pears, rubbing them with lemon juice and sprinkling with 1 teaspoon sugar.

✓ In a saucepan, put cinnamon, coriander, Szechuan pepper, cloves, remaining sugar, lemon zest, and orange slice with 2 cups water. Bring to a boil, add pear halves, and poach for 5–15 minutes, until they yield to a fork. Let cool completely in the syrup.

✓ In a small saucepan, bring 1 cup water to a boil, blanch lardons briefly. Drain and cool.

✓ Preheat oven to 400°F.

✓ Cut the round of Fourme de Montbrison into 4 equal wedges.

✓ Roll out puff pastry, cut 4 equal 5-inch squares, and place on a baking sheet. On each pastry square lay a wedge of cheese at an angle, an inch from the edge, then add a pear half, strew with lardons, and dust with curry powder. Bake 10–15 minutes. Serve.

A green salad with walnut oil dressing makes a good accompaniment.

Serves 4
2 Bartlett pears
1 lemon, zested
1/3 cup sugar
1 cinnamon stick
8 coriander seeds
8 Szechuan peppercorns
2 cloves
1 slice orange
2 ounces small bacon cubes
1 finger-thick slice Fourme de Montbrison, or other blue cheese, about 1/2 pound
1 sheet puff pastry
Curry powder for dusting

Fondue in a Fourme de Montbrison
Fondue à la Fourme de Montbrison

"Today the Fourme de Montbrison is produced by two industrial firms, Forez Fourme and the Laiterie du Pont de la Pierre run by Lactalis; by the artisanal cheesemaker Hubert Tarit, using locally collected milk and traditional methods; and by the Plagne family of Sauvain on their farm."

Régis Juanico
Deputy of Loire

Serves 4
1 whole Fourme de Montbrison,
about 4 pounds
2/3 cup heavy cream
3/4 cup dry white wine,
preferably Chardonnay
2 pounds fingerling potatoes,
boiled
Assorted cold cuts

✓ Cut the fourme in two, crosswise. Spoon out the insides from each of the open cylinders, making sure to leave the shell intact.
✓ In a saucepan, melt the spooned-out cheese in the cream and wine, stirring constantly until smooth. Season to taste.
✓ Pour cheese back into the two crusts. Set one fondue between each pair of diners.

Serve along with boiled potatoes, to be dipped in the fondue, and charcuterie.

Salmon Filets with Sorrel
Escalopes de saumon à l'oseille

Roanne, a large town in the Loire department less than sixty miles northwest of Lyons, is known for both industry and agriculture and, more recently, for its famous restaurant Les Frères Troisgros.

"Why salmon in Roanne? you might ask. It all goes back to the nineteenth century when the soft water of the Loire proved beneficial to textile manufacture in Roanne. Another important local industry was river transport. Salmon was so abundant in the Loire, we are told, it became the standard fare of barge crews—so much so that they went on strike to protest finding salmon in their lunch pails day in and day out.

"Since then, much water has run under the Roanne bridge. And the local salmon has long since disappeared. But in the 1970s the brothers Jean and Pierre Troisgros perfected this recipe and added to their international fame. With three consistent Michelin stars since 1968, La Maison Troisgros in the hands of Pierre's son Michel today is carrying on the brilliant family gastronomic tradition."

Yves Nicolin
Deputy of Loire

<u>Serves 4</u>
2 salmon filets (about 2 pounds)
2 cups fresh sorrel
1 cup fish stock
1/2 cup white wine, preferably Sancerre
1/4 cup dry vermouth
2 shallots, minced
2 cups crème fraiche
1/2 lemon
Pepper and salt

✓ With tweezers, remove bones. To ensure that all bones are out, run your fingers against the grain. With a sharp knife, cut filets horizontally into 4 escalopes. Place each escalope between parchment paper, and pound gently so the pieces are of uniform thickness.

✓ Remove stems from sorrel. Wash leaves, and tear up the larger ones.

✓ In a small sauté pan, combine fish stock, wine, vermouth, and shallots. Cook down to a syrupy consistency. Stir in crème fraiche and let it boil for 5 seconds. Throw in the sorrel and cook 15 seconds more, swirling the pan. Add a few drops of lemon juice, and season to taste. Reserve, keeping warm.

✓ Set 4 plates in a warming oven.

✓ Sprinkle pepper and salt on salmon escalopes. Heat a large skillet (if nonstick, without fat; if not, with a few drops of oil). Sauté salmon 25 seconds on one side, 15 seconds on the other. Salmon must be pink inside.

✓ Divide sauce between heated plates, placing sautéd salmon over sauce. Serve immediately.

Creamed Mushrooms
Marinière de charbonniers

"I was born in a small village 4,300 feet up in the mountains of the Auvergne, surrounded by meadows and forests, and always marveled at our lush and rich environment. Going out and picking mushrooms was one of my childhood pleasures. It made me feel important bringing my bounty home to my mother, who would turn it into a delicious dish for her restaurant. Years later my brother's restaurant at Saint-Bonnet-le-Froid has garnered three Michelin stars. And, like my mother, his motto has always been to bring together our local products, our herbs, and our mushrooms. I thank him for this simple and savory recipe."

Jean-Pierre Marcon
Deputy of Haute-Loire

The charbonnier *or* tricholome prétentieux *is a gray-capped, umbrella-shaped mushroom related to the* mousseron *that grows in layers, on tree logs. To approximate the* charbonniers, *substitute a mix of chanterelles and cremini.*

✓ Prepare *charbonnier* mushrooms: Cut off caps and peel them. Wipe well. If using chanterelles and cremini, simply cut off stem tip and wipe with a dry cloth or paper towel.

✓ In a large skillet, heat olive oil and butter. Sauté shallots 5 minutes, add mushrooms, cook another 5 minutes. Add pepper and salt. Pour in wine, cover, and cook over low heat for 20 minutes. The mushrooms will give up their liquid.

✓ Meanwhile, mix together softened butter, flour, parsley, and garlic.

✓ Drain sautéd mushrooms in a sieve over a saucepan. Place drained mushrooms in a serving bowl and keep warm.

✓ In the saucepan, bring the mushroom liquid to a boil, whisk in the parsley butter, and continue whisking 3–4 minutes until sauce becomes velvety. Adjust seasoning. Pour sauce over mushrooms and serve.

Serves 4

1–2 pounds mushrooms
1 tablespoon olive oil
4 tablespoons butter
3 shallots, minced
Pepper and salt
1/2 cup dry white wine

For the parsley butter:
6 tablespoon butter, softened
1 tablespoon flour
1/2 cup parsley, finely chopped
1 garlic clove, minced

Oysters Four Ways, from the Pays de Retz

Huitres des quatre saisons du pays de Retz

The coastal department of Loire-Atlantique is the southernmost part of the historical region of Brittany. The Pays de Retz is the area south of the estuary of the Loire.

"This part of France is so rich in natural products, it wasn't easy to choose. Being an unconditional seafood lover, however, I opted for oysters. Most people enjoy their oysters raw with lemon juice or ravigote or mignonette sauce, accompanied by Muscadet wine, brown bread, and butter. I have a weakness for winter oysters with their stronger taste of iodine. When I eat them and close my eyes, I am transported right back to the Breton beaches with my feet in sand.

"Here I offer four variations on the oyster theme, one to suggest each season."

Philippe Boennec
Deputy of Loire-Atlantique

Serves 4

Winter
8 oysters, shucked, shells and liquor reserved
Juice of 1/2 lemon
1/4 cup Gros Plant Nantais, or other white Loire Valley wine

Spring
8 oysters, shucked, liquor reserved
1 cauliflower
1 tablespoon heavy cream
1 tablespoon gelatin powder

Summer
8 oysters, shucked, liquor reserved
1/4 cup olive oil
1 small bunch scallions, thinly sliced
1 shallot, finely chopped
1 tablespoon butter
1/2 cup Gros Plant
1 sprig lemon thyme

Fall
8 oysters, shucked, liquor reserved
1/4 cup heavy cream
1/2 teaspoon curry powder
12 cumin seeds
1 tablespoon butter

WINTER: OYSTER ICE

✓ In a blender, purée oysters, lemon juice, wine, and oyster liquor. Pour into a metal bowl and place in freezer, mixing gently every 30 minutes. If you have an ice cream maker, follow instructions.

✓ Serve in wide champagne coupes, with a scrubbed oyster shell to use as a spoon.

SPRING: CHAUD-FROID OF CAULIFLOWER WITH OYSTERS

✓ Boil cauliflower 10 minutes. Purée in blender with 1/4 cup oyster liquor, filtered. Add cream and pepper. On a serving plate, shape cauliflower purée into a flat cake. Chill.

✓ Dilute gelatin with 1/2 cup oyster liquor. Heat to dissolve, then chill. When it is thickened to the consistency of egg white, coat the cauliflower with the aspic. Return to refrigerator until set. Place oysters on top and serve.

SUMMER: OYSTERS HEATED À LA MARINIÈRE

✓ Reduce oyster liquor to 1/4 cup. Whisk briskly with olive oil. Add scallions. Reserve.

✓ In a pan, sauté shallots in butter. Add wine and lemon thyme, and bring to a boil. Stir in oil mixture.

✓ Place hot liquid in a bowl and add oysters until they warm through but do not cook. Serve.

FALL: OYSTERS IN A WARM CURRY

✓ Turn on the broiler. In a pan, heat 1 tablespoon oyster liquor, cream, curry, and cumin. Do not let it boil. Place oysters in their shells on a cookie sheet. Pour sauce over oysters, and broil for a mere few seconds, no more. Serve immediately.

Praline Ice Cream
Glace "Au duc de Praslin"

The Loiret department, in the heart of the Loire valley, takes its name from a very short but lovely tributary that flows into the Loire near the regional capital, Orléans. The department's second city, Montargis, farther east, is barely a hundred kilometers from Paris. The Loiret is notably rich in agriculture, industry, tourism—and gastronomy.
"From an original recipe using Spanish almonds, this ice cream based on powdered pralines was developed by Léon Mazet, confectioner of the celebrated Mazet de Montargis pralines. Enjoy in serenity!"

Jean-Pierre Door
Deputy of Loiret

✔ Reduce the pralines to powder, pausing in the middle of the process to set aside about an ounce of good-sized chips for decoration.

✔ In a heavy saucepan, lightly beat the egg yolks and work the praline powder in, combining well. Separately, heat the milk just to a boil. Add it bit by bit to the yolk mixture, stirring constantly. Set the saucepan over low heat, still stirring, until bubbles first appear, then remove immediately.

✔ When this custard has cooled, beat in the cream. If you have an ice cream machine, freeze according to instructions. If not, turn the mixture into one or more molds. Place in the freezer. Until the freezing is well advanced, mix gently every 30 minutes.

✔ Half an hour before serving time, remove from freezer. To serve, invert and unmold. Sprinkle with the reserved praline bits.

Variation: Before freezing, you may add ladyfingers soaked in Cointreau or Grand Marnier.

Serves 8–10 (makes 1 liter)
9 ounces pralines
8 egg yolks
1 cup milk
1 cup crème fraiche

Almond Cake
Pithiviers fondant

The whole Loiret department prides itself on being very fertile as well as a gastronomic center. Pithiviers, in the northern part, is known for its galette des rois, which appears in all its pastry shops at Epiphany—the feast of Three Kings, the twelfth day of Christmas. All year long, the name Pithiviers is synonymous with a two-crust puff pastry tart, filled usually with almond paste. And then there is the dessert below, not a tart but a cake. For a town with such culinary connotations, it is perhaps fitting that Pithiviers is located on the river Oeuf.

"This Pithiviers specialty, so delicious and rich in flavors, is actually extremely simple to make. When my mother and my grandmother baked it, they would accompany it with a vanilla custard, crème anglaise."

Marianne Dubois
Deputy of Loiret

Serves 6–8

1/2 pound almond flour
1 cup granulated sugar
5 eggs
2 sticks butter, softened
2 tablespoons cornstarch
1 tablespoon rum
2 cups confectioners' sugar
Candied fruits (optional)

✓ Butter a cake pan or a charlotte mold. Preheat oven to 350°F.

✓ In a large bowl, combine almond flour and granulated sugar, then stir in eggs one by one. The mixture will have a sandy texture.

✓ Melt butter and stir in, along with cornstarch and rum.

✓ Pour into buttered pan. Bake 30—35 minutes. Be careful not to overbake: the cake should be very soft. Remove and allow to cool.

✓ In a bowl, mix confectioners' sugar with 2 tablespoons hot water to make an icing. Spread over cooled cake. Decorate if desired with candied fruits.

Variation: For a festive occasion, you may bake individual cakes in small molds and arrange them in an attractive tier. Remember, though, to reduce the cooking time accordingly.

Perch in a Vinegar Sauce

Sandre de Loire au vinaigre d'Orleans

The Loiret department's capital, Orléans, was already historically important for a millennium and a half before Joan of Arc led the French to victory there in 1429 and effectively turned the tide of the Hundred Years War.

"Orléans has been considered the Vinegar Capital since the eighteenth century, when Martin Pouret's family firm made its name with the production of vinegar by a unique and closely guarded traditional method. Since the year 2001, our city has worked to reestablish fishing in the Loire. This is what inspired me to offer this delicious recipe that celebrates both our patrimony and our geography."

Serge Grouard
Deputy of Loiret

✓ Ask the fishmonger to scale the fish and remove the bones from the filets.
✓ Fill a kettle halfway with water. Bring water to a boil, cook cabbage 2 minutes. Remove and immerse cabbage in a bowl of ice water. Drain. Chop cabbage roughly.
✓ In a heavy casserole, sauté lardons gently. When they have rendered much of their fat, remove and reserve.
✓ In the bacon fat, toss cabbage and cook over medium heat 30 minutes, until it cooks down to a compote. Stir occasionally and add a little water if it looks like it might burn.
✓ Preheat oven to 400°F.
✓ Pepper and salt the skinless side of the fish filets. Rub skin side with olive oil. In a skillet, sauté fish on skin side 2 minutes. Remove fish to a baking sheet, and finish in the oven, about 5 minutes.
✓ In the skillet, place the reserved lardons and stir to rewarm and crisp for a few minutes. Pour vinegar in pan, scrape to deglaze, and stir in cream. Season to taste.
✓ Divide cabbage compote on serving plates, place filets over compote, and cover with sauce.

Serves 4

4 pike perch filets
1 Savoy cabbage, cut into 4 pieces
1/4 pound bacon cubes (lardons)
Pepper and salt
2 tablespoons olive oil
1 cup wine vinegar, preferably à l'ancienne from Orléans
1 cup heavy cream

Serve immediately, with a well-chilled Sancerre.

Pastry Rolled around Pear and Apple

Pastis du Quercy

The Lot department in the southwest of France, part of the old province of Languedoc, is named after its river Lot, a tributary of the Garonne. The Lot produces wine, especially around Cahors, and a full range of foodstuffs. Pastis here is not the anise-flavored aperitif popular in southern France, but a supremely delicate pastry. It is also a word meaning "a sticky situation."

"Our pastis is one of the most emblematic and most delectable desserts from a long Quercy tradition. This aromatic, crisp yet melt-in-your-mouth recipe used to be passed down from mother to daughter. Nowadays it is seldom made, for it takes a lot of time and attention to detail. An extremely thin dough flavored with eau-de-vie is stretched into a long sheet before assembling the pastry with slices of apple and pear. Patience is needed, and elbow room, and of course a serious touch of gourmandise."

Dominique Orliac
Deputy of Lot

Serves 7–8

6 cups flour
4 eggs
pinch of salt
2 cups warm water
8 tablespoons butter
1/2 cup canola oil
1 apple
1 pear
1 tablespoon orange flower water
2 tablespoons eau-de-vie
2 tablespoons vanilla extract
1 cup sugar

✓ In a large bowl, put the flour and salt, make a well in the center of the flour, and crack the eggs into it. Slowly pouring in the warm water, work the mixture into a soft, smooth dough. This must be done long and thoroughly, so as to incorporate air, which will allow the dough to develop. Cover with film, and let rest 3 hours.

✓ Lay a fine tablecloth or bedsheet over a large table, ideally 6 feet square. Place the dough in the center of the cloth. It will begin to spread by itself. Slide your hands underneath the cloth and work the dough, nudging it outward with your fingers until it gradually covers the whole work surface in a very thin layer, like cigarette paper. Let it rest 10 minutes.

✓ Preheat oven to 350°F.

✓ Melt butter and mix with oil. With a pastry brush, paint the dough sheet entirely.

✓ Peel and core the apple and pear. Slice very finely. Place fruit evenly over dough.

✓ In a small bowl, combine orange flower water, eau-de-vie, and vanilla. Sprinkle the entire surface with this liquid, then with sugar.

✓ Grasping one edge of the cloth and lifting, lightly roll the filled dough onto itself to form a tube. Do not tamp down, just keep it rolling by gathering up the cloth. Delicately place the tube, in a spiral, in a round, high baking dish, preferably with a cover.

✓ Bake 20 minutes uncovered until the pastry is nicely colored. Then cover the dish and continue baking 20 minutes more. Remove from oven, unmold, cut into pieces, and serve warm.

Poached Chicken with Stuffing and Rich Rice
Poule au pot et sa farce avec du riz au gras

"Try to buy a nice, plump hen from a farmers' market. Though fowl today are sold already cleaned, make sure you get the giblets for the stuffing. The poule au pot *is not merely a good dish, it symbolizes the joy of conviviality, from a happy country where sharing supersedes dietetic concerns."*

Michel Diefenbacher
Deputy of Lot-et-Garonne

Serves 6–8
1 5-pound chicken
10 garlic cloves, peeled
Pork rind, enough to line the pot
2 onions, peeled and quartered
3 leeks, well washed, cut into
2-inch chunks
4–5 carrots, peeled and sliced
thickly
5 turnips, peeled and quartered
10 potatoes, peeled and halved
1 can tomato paste
1 bouquet garni (parsley, celery,
bay leaf)
Pepper and salt
For the stuffing:
Liver and gizzard of chicken
1 pound pork sausage meat
1 pound stale bread, soaked in
water and squeezed dry
6 eggs
Pepper and salt

✓ Start by preparing the stuffing. In the food processor, grind the liver and gizzard. Place them in a bowl with the sausage meat, eggs, bread, pepper, and salt, and mix well. Reserve a small handful for stuffing the bird, and shape the rest of the stuffing into a ball. Enclose it in a sturdy piece of cloth and tie it like a purse with kitchen twine.
✓ Place garlic cloves and reserved stuffing inside chicken. Sew or skewer the opening securely.
✓ In a kettle, line bottom with pork rinds. Place purse of stuffing and chicken on top of rind. Add vegetables, tomato paste, and bouquet garni. Cover with water, at least 2 inches above ingredients. Cook 1 hour over medium heat, reduce to low, and simmer for 1 hour more.
✓ Remove from heat. Taste and adjust seasoning. Cool. Refrigerate at least 5 hours, preferably overnight. A layer of fat will come to the surface. Lift it off and reserve it.
✓ Cook rice, using the chicken fat and sufficient broth from the pot instead of water. The rice will swell greatly and be very delicious, served with the broth, chicken, sliced stuffing, and vegetables. The broth may be served alone first, or in a soup plate along with the rest.

"We drink a wine from Duras in the Lot-et-Garonne with our poule au pot.*"*

Agen Prunes on Coconut Cream with Armagnac

Pruneau d'Agen au plat

Prunes from the Agen region have been a prized part of the culinary heritage of southwestern France for centuries. They are particularly tasty, juicy, and plump.
"This recipe was developed with the participation of the chef Eric Mariottat, restaurateur in the town of Agen."

Jean Dionis du Séjour
Deputy of Lot-et-Garonne

✓ Make a sugar syrup from 1 cup water and 1/2 cup sugar. Boil, reduce heat, and simmer to thicken. Add prunes and tea bag. Simmer 5 minutes. Turn heat off, and let steep 10 minutes. Remove prunes and reserve.
✓ Make the coconut cream. In a pan, heat glucose and 1 cup water with softened gelatin. When dissolved, stir in coconut milk. Cool, refrigerate, then strain through a fine sieve. Divide coconut cream between 4 dessert bowls. Keep cold.
✓ Pit the prunes, chop them finely, and stir in enough Armagnac to make a smooth paste. At serving time, place a mound of puréed prune mixture in the center of each dish. It should look like a fried egg.
✓ Serve cold.

Serves 4
8 large Agen prunes
1/2 cup sugar
1 tea bag
2 ounces glucose
2 tablespoons gelatin
2 cups coconut milk
1/4 cup Armagnac

Prune Pudding
Coupétado

"A delight at the end of a meal, or at breakfast, or at five-o'clock tea, this amalgam of bread and fruit is a subtle blend of savory and sweet. The coupétado is named for the coupet, *the deep earthenware vessel in which this dessert was traditionally baked."*

Pierre Morel À l'Huissier
Deputy of Lozère

Serves 10

20 pruneaux d'Agen, or other large prunes, pitted
1/2 cup raisins
10 slices day-old bread
4 cups milk
5 eggs
1/2 cup sugar
1 teaspoon vanilla extract

✓ Preheat oven to 375°F.
✓ Butter an ovenproof baking dish. Distribute prunes and raisins as bottom layer. Cover fruit with bread slices. Leave a good inch between bread and edges of baking dish, as the bread will almost double in size.
✓ In a bowl, whisk milk, eggs, sugar, and vanilla until smooth and uniform. Pour over bread slices. Press down with a fork, so that all the bread is soaked in liquid.
✓ Bake for 1 hour, or until the pudding is puffed up and nicely browned.

Serve warm or cold. May be topped with a caramel sauce or with whipped cream.

White Mousse with Raspberry Coulis

Crémet d'Anjou

The Maine-et-Loire department is in the old province of Anjou. Many say that its capital, Angers, the medieval seat of the Plantagenets, with its twelfth-century cathedral and its seventeen-tower castle housing magnificent tapestries, is one of the most beautiful cities in France.

One specialty of the region of Anjou is this traditional dessert concocted of whipped cream and whipped egg white, often accompanied by fresh fruits of the season.

"The crémet is at once light and luxurious. I like it especially served with a raspberry coulis."

Paul Jeanneteau
Deputy of Maine-et-Loire

✓ To make the coulis, purée raspberries with sugar in the blender. Reserve.

✓ In a chilled bowl, whip the cream. In a dry bowl, whip the egg whites until they form soft peaks. Mix the two with a whisk.

✓ Line a colander with cheesecloth and place it over a bowl. Put the mousse into the colander and tamp it down. Refrigerate 2 hours or more.

✓ In a small bowl, mix sugar and vanilla sugar.

✓ At serving time, remove colander from refrigerator, invert a rimmed dish over it, and flip to unmold the *crémet*. Peel off the cheesecloth. Pour raspberry coulis over *crémet*, and bring to table.

✓ Serve in individual dessert dishes, passing the sugar bowl separately.

Variation: When berries are out of season, the *crémet* can simply be topped with crème fraiche and the vanilla sugar, for an all-white presentation.

Serves 4
1 cup heavy cream
2 egg whites
1/3 cup sugar
1 tablespoon vanilla sugar
For the coulis:
2 cups raspberries
1/3 cup sugar

Chicken Poached and Sauteed with Chanterelles

Volaille d'Anjou "pochée rôtie"aux girolles des bois de Beaufort

"My great friends Sébastien and Gérard Girardeau of Saumur— award-winning specialists in preparing pig's feet—who never lack creative ideas to enhance the bounties of Anjou, shared their recipe with me. Every year, as soon as the chanterelles spring up, I join them in mushroom hunting in Beaufort-en-Vallée and return home with my basket full, ready to concoct this wonderful dish of Anjou chicken."

Jean-Charles Tangourdeau
Deputy of Maine-et-Loire

Serves 4

1 pound chanterelles
1 5-pound chicken
Pepper and salt
1 carrot, peeled
1 leek, white only, well washed
1 onion, peeled
3 cloves garlic
2 sprigs thyme
1 egg yolk
10 tablespoons butter
1 tablespoon olive oil
2 shallots, minced

✓ Sort mushrooms, wash in several waters, and set on absorbent paper to dry.

✓ Wash chicken under running water, inside and out. Pepper and salt inside. Truss.

✓ In a large kettle, put 6 quarts water with the carrot, leek, onion, 2 cloves garlic, 1 sprig thyme, and some salt. Bring to a boil for 15 minutes, then reduce heat to a simmer. Add chicken and cook for 30 minutes. Turn heat off and let chicken rest in the stock for another 20 minutes.

✓ Over a saucepan, place a sieve and strain 4 cups of the stock. Reduce stock over brisk heat to 1 cup liquid. Off heat, add egg yolk and 6 tablespoons butter. With a whisk or in the blender, create an emulsion. Keep warm.

✓ Carve chicken into serving pieces. In a skillet, melt 3 tablespoons butter. Brown the pieces of poached chicken. Place on a serving platter and keep warm.

✓ In a skillet, heat olive oil and 1 tablespoon butter. Mince remaining clove garlic and sauté until golden. Stir in chanterelles and leaves stripped from remaining sprig of thyme. Season chanterelles and add shallots. Continue stirring for 5 minutes.

✓ Place chanterelles over browned chicken pieces on the platter. Coat with sauce and serve.

Norman Poached Chicken with Chestnuts

Poule au blanc à la normande

The Manche department, named after the body of water the French call La Manche (the Sleeve) and the British call the English Channel, is the westernmost in Normandy. At its head is the port of Cherbourg and at its foot, almost in Brittany, is the magical Mont Saint-Michel. Almost everything in between is farmland.
"This traditional dish is among the classics of Lower Normandy cuisine that I have enjoyed since early childhood at Sunday dinners around the family table. The recipe is still very much in favor today throughout our region. My own version, cooked in the oven, also has the virtue of being simple to prepare."

Alain Cousin
Deputy of Manche

Serves 6–8

1 organic chicken
Pepper and salt
1 sprig parsley
1 cup sweet cider
1 onion, peeled and quartered
2 garlic cloves
4 carrots, peeled, whole
4 leeks, washed, trimmed
1 celery stalk with leaves
3 turnips, peeled and trimmed
4 sprigs thyme
1 bay leaf
2 pounds chestnuts, cooked and peeled
Zest of 1 lemon
1 cup heavy cream
Juice of 1/2 lemon
1 teaspoon quatre-épices (blend of ground clove, ginger, nutmeg, and white pepper)
1/2 cup parsley, finely scissored

✓ Preheat oven to 350°F.
✓ Wash chicken under running water, inside and out. Season all sides and the interior, and insert a sprig of parsley in the cavity.
✓ In a kettle, place the chicken with 3 cups water, the cider, onions, garlic, carrots, leeks, celery, turnips, thyme, bay leaf, and some salt. Cover, place in oven, and cook 2 hours. Check occasionally and add water if need be.
✓ Toward the end of the 2 hours, add chestnuts and lemon zest, and adjust seasoning. Cook an additional 15 minutes.
✓ Remove from oven. Stir in cream, lemon juice, and quatre-épices. Sprinkle with parsley and serve.

Ramequins of Andouille in Apple Wine and Camembert

Petites cocottes normandes à l'andouille de Vire, au pommeau et camembert

"Fairly simple to prepare, this dish places on display much of our region's bounty—andouilles from Vire, apples, crème fraiche, our camembert, our typical apple wine called pommeau—all products that are the pride of Normandy. Pommeau is made of apples mixed with calvados, our fine apple brandy, and aged in oak barrels for a year and a half. It has a slight fruity scent, and an amber color.
"This recipe can be made well in advance, and actually 'seasons' advantageously while sitting. It shines in a variety of roles. It is a main course; served in smaller portions, it becomes an appetizer; and I have often seen it served at cocktail parties, as a hot hors d'oeuvre, in a large spoon."

Philippe Gosselin
Deputy of the Manche

✓ Preheat oven to 425°F.
✓ In a skillet, melt 3 tablespoons butter. Sauté shallots 10 minutes, until translucent. Add flour and stir while it cooks in, then gradually pour in pommeau wine, stirring constantly over low heat for 10 minutes to obtain a smooth and thick sauce. Add diced ham and andouille, and parsley. Simmer for a few minutes, watching that it does not stick. Add both creams and stir gently until sauce is smooth. Season to taste. Set aside.
✓ Peel and core the apple, and cut it into 1/2-inch cubes. In a nonstick skillet, melt remaining 2 tablespoons butter and toss apple cubes over high heat so that they brown without collapsing. Add apples to sauced preparation. It should be somewhat cooled but not cold..
✓ In a soufflé dish, or 4 small individual ones, put the sauced preparation. Add a layer of camembert slices. Cover and bake about 10 minutes. Remove from oven a few minutes before serving.

Optional: Instead of placing a cover on each ramequin, you can add a lid of puff pastry and bake about 15 minutes or until pastry is golden brown.

Serves 4

5 tablespoons butter
2 shallots, finely chopped
2 tablespoons flour
1 1/2 cups pommeau
2 cups ham, diced
1 cup andouille de Vire (can be ordered at specialty stores), diced
2 tablespoons parsley, finely chopped
2/3 cup heavy cream
3–4 tablespoons crème fraiche
Pepper and salt
1 large apple
1 ripe camembert, peeled and sliced
Puff pastry (optional)

Braised Beef, Tongue, Pork, Sausages, and Vegetables
Potée champenoise

"The northeastern Marne department is traversed east-to-west by the river Marne, the principal tributary of the Seine. Reims possesses a magnificent Gothic cathedral, Romanesque basilica, and other attractions. But for gastronomes, the Marne's main claim to attention is its champagne vineyards.

"This seasonal dish is the meal traditionally served to the grape pickers in the fall. One of its virtues is that it simmers for hours, needing little tending, which permits the mistress of the household to go off and tend to other duties."

Catherine Vautrin
Deputy of Marne

Serves 10

1 pound dried white beans
2 pounds beef short ribs
1 beef tongue
1 salted pork shoulder, or smoked picnic shoulder
1 pound pork belly
1 large onion, peeled and studded with 6 cloves
1 bouquet garni
Peppercorns
20 carrots
10 turnips
3 leeks
1 celery stalk
1 Savoy cabbage, quartered
5 smoked pork or turkey sausages, such as kielbasa
20 potatoes
1 pound vermicelli

✓ Soak the dried beans overnight.
✓ In a large kettle, put beef, tongue, pork shoulder, pork belly, onion, bouquet garni, and peppercorns. Cover with cold water. Bring to a boil, reduce heat to a simmer, and cook 1 1/2 hours, skimming surface at the beginning.
✓ Add carrots, turnips, leeks, and celery, and cook an additional 1 1/2 hours.
✓ Drain the soaked beans and add, along with sausages and cabbage. Continue cooking another 30 minutes.
✓ Add potatoes. Cook 30 minutes more. Adjust seasoning.
✓ Remove most of broth to a smaller pot and cook vermicelli in it. Serve as first course.
✓ Serve meats and vegetables, accompanied by mustard.

The next day, leftover vegetables may be cut small and sautéed in butter. Leftover tongue may be served in a sauce piquant (brown sauce with pickles and capers), or a fresh tomato sauce.

Profiteroles Filled with Langres Cheese
Profiteroles de langres

Make no mistake. These profiteroles are not a dessert. The little choux pastries are filled with the the local Langres, a soft cheese that resembles the Époisses of neighboring Burgundy. Made from cow's milk, with a washed yellow-orange rind and a slightly sunken top, the spicy Langres melts in your mouth when it is enjoyed at its best, between May and August, after five to six weeks of aging. This recipe was provided by Sophie Delong, deputy of Haute-Marne.

Serves 4
3 tablespoons butter
2 shallots, minced
3/4 cup white wine
1/2 cup chicken stock
2 Langres cheeses, about 6 ounces each
1/2 cup heavy cream
1 teaspoon potato starch or cornstarch
For the choux pastry:
1/2 cup water
1/2 stick butter
1/2 cup flour
3 eggs

✓ Preheat oven to 375°F.

✓ Prepare the choux pastry. In a pan, bring to a boil water and butter. Turn heat off. Quickly add flour, stirring vigorously until dough forms and becomes smooth. Stir in eggs, one by one. On a cookie sheet lined with buttered parchment paper, drop 12 little mounds, at least 1 inch apart. Bake 30 minutes until choux puff up. Remove from oven. Cool.

✓ In a saucepan, melt butter and sauté shallots until golden. Pour in white wine and cook to reduce by a third. Add chicken stock and simmer 15 minutes. Cut up 1 Langres cheese, add to stock, and stir until it melts. In a small bowl, dilute starch with cream and add to saucepan. Stir steadily with a whisk until the sauce is smooth and shiny. Keep warm over simmering water.

✓ Slice second Langres cheese into 12 pieces.

✓ With a serrated knife, cut off tops of choux. If needed, scrape out little bits of uncooked dough inside choux, and discard. Stuff each chou with 1 piece cheese. Replace tops of choux. Return the 12 choux to 375°F oven and bake 5–8 minutes to melt cheese.

Serve hot, 2 choux on a plate, coated with warm cheese sauce. Accompany with a green salad.

Apple Terrine in Cider Aspic with Caramel

Terrine de pommes au cidre et fine du Maine et son caramel normand

Mayenne, in the Loire country in northwestern France, is named after the river Mayenne, which flows south to join the Sarthe and form to the river Maine. The district called the Maine, however, is in the departments of Mayenne and Sarthe, well north of the Maine River. The naming of French geography is sometimes full of twists, like its rivers. "Eau-de-vie is a product produced particularly in the northern part of the Mayenne department, and has become increasingly rare these days. Hard cider, also a local product, is enjoyed by the Mayennais, as our region, like neighboring Normandy, is filled with apple orchards. The fine du Maine *brandy is distilled from hard cider and aged in oak barrels."*

Marc Bernier
Deputy of Mayenne

✓ Peel and core the apples and cut in 1/2-inch cubes.
✓ In a skillet, over medium heat, melt butter and cook apples with orange zest and juice until lightly caramelized. Pour in brandy, ignite, and let flames subside.
✓ In a small bowl, dilute gelatin with 3 tablespoons cold water.
✓ In a saucepan, cook cider with sugar until reduced by half. Off heat, stir in gelatin.
✓ Spread cooked apples in a flat-bottomed, straight-sided dish and pour cider gelatin over apples. Refrigerate for 24 hours.
✓ In a saucepan, heat cider and sugar, cooking until it turns light brown. Stir in cream gradually, let boil for 1 minute, then cool. Reserve.
✓ Unmold apple aspic and serve covered with cider caramel sauce.

Serves 6

5 Granny Smith apples
2 tablespoons butter
Zest and juice of 1 orange
1/4 cup apple brandy
3/4 cup sugar
1 cup hard cider
2 tablespoons gelatin

For the Norman caramel:
1/4 cup sugar
2 tablespoons hard cider
1/4 cup heavy cream

Blue Cake
Gâteau bleu

Located in France's northeastern corner, Lorraine, the department of Meurthe-et-Moselle takes its name from two rivers that rise in the Vosges Mountains just to the south.

"I am offering an original Lorraine recipe inspired by the cakes my grandparents used to serve us in my childhood, using ingredients native to our Lorraine region, notably the blueberries that grow there in abundance."

Laurent Hénart
Deputy of Meurthe-et-Moselle

Serves 4
For the génoise:
2 eggs
1/3 cup sugar
1/3 cup flour
2 tablespoons cornstarch

For the blueberry cream:
3 egg yolks
1/4 cup sugar
1 tablespoon flour
1 tablespoon cornstarch
1 1/2 cups warm milk
1 teaspoon vanilla extract
1 tablespoon butter
1 tablespoon gelatin
2 cups blueberries
1 cup heavy cream

For the icing:
2/3 cup white chocolate
1/2 cup strained blueberry juice

✔ For the génoise, preheat oven to 350°F. Butter and flour 2 cake pans. In a bowl, whisk eggs and sugar until pale and fluffy. Add sifted flour and cornstarch. Pour half the mixture in each pan. Bake 20–25 minutes or until knife inserted in center comes out clean. Remove from oven. Cool.

✔ For the blueberry cream, make a crème pâtissière: In a bowl, whip egg yolks, sugar, flour, and cornstarch until pale and creamy. Stir in warm milk. Cook over low heat, stirring, until thickened. Add vanilla. Off heat, stir in butter. Cool.

✔ Soften the gelatin in a bit of water.

✔ Blend 2/3 cup blueberries and strain. Reserve half for the icing.

✔ In a chilled bowl, whip the cream. Mix in the gelatin and half the blueberry juice. Incorporate in crème pâtissière. Chill.

✔ To prepare the icing, in a small saucepan (or a glass, in the microwave) melt remaining blueberry juice with white chocolate.

✔ Now assemble the cake. Fold blueberries into cream mixture. On a cake plate, place one layer of génoise. Spread with blueberry cream. Top with second layer of génoise. Spread icing over top and sides of cake.

For decoration, you can add leftover blue icing, chilled and shaved, or more fresh blueberries.

Meat Pie from Lorraine

Tourte lorraine

"The tourte lorraine *is a pie with not one but two different pastry crusts, filled with meat marinated in either white wine or rosé. While it takes just an hour to bake the tourte, the meat does need to rest for six hours in the marinade beforehand. I picked this typical recipe, less known than the famous* pâté lorrain, *because it reminds me of the Sunday evenings of my childhood when my grandmother prepared it for us, accompanied by a green salad."*

Philippe Morenvillier
Deputy of Meurthe-et-Moselle

Serves 4

1 pound boneless pork ribs, cut in thin strips

1 pound boneless veal roast, diced

Pâte brisée for a 1-crust pie (page 3)

Puff pastry for a 1-crust pie

4 eggs

1 cup milk

1 cup light cream

For the marinade:

1 bottle Riesling or other dry white wine

1 onion, studded with 4 cloves

3 garlic cloves, minced

1 bay leaf

1 bunch parsley, chopped

2 shallots, minced

1 teaspoon salt

Pepper

✓ In a bowl, pour half the wine and add all the other marinade ingredients. Toss meats in it, adding wine to cover. Place in plastic bags, seal, and refrigerate for 6 hours.

✓ Take pâte brisée from the refrigerator.

✓ Preheat oven to 400°F. Roll out pâte brisée and fit into a deep tart mold, leaving a border overhanging. Remove meat from marinade and place over pie dough. Salt and pepper.

✓ Roll out puff pastry. Cut a circle larger than the mold. Lay gently over meat. Seal the two pastries by moistening edges and crimping with fingers tightly. In the center, cut a small hole. With a knife, crosshatch the pastry or make a design of your choice.

✓ Beat the yolk of one egg with a little water. With a pastry brush, paint top crust. Place tourte in oven for 25 minutes.

✓ Meanwhile, make a *migaine* (quiche filling, in Lorraine). In a bowl, mix 3 eggs, milk, cream, and a little salt.

✓ Remove tourte and lower oven setting to 375°F. Pour *migaine* into tourte through a funnel inserted in the hole. Put back in oven for another 25–30 minutes, or until cooked through.

Serve hot or cold.

Red Currant Tart with Meringue

Tarte meringuée aux groseilles de mon jardin

In the Meuse department, bordering on Belgium, many names—Verdun, Saint-Mihiel, Argonne Forest—still evoke the fearful slaughter of the First World War. More tranquil today, the river Meuse gains volume in France to wind northward through the Low Countries where, its name changed to the Maas, it becomes a major means of transport. "This tart is always a success. If fresh currants are out of season, it can be made with frozen fruit. It can be eaten warm but is best enjoyed cold, with a well-chilled red currant wine."

Bertrand Pancher
Deputy of Meuse

✓ Preheat oven to 375°F.

✓ Strip the currants from their stems into a sieve, wash, and leave to drain.

✓ In a skillet over high heat, toast the powdered nuts or coconut. Set aside.

✓ Roll out dough and line a tart mold. Prick with a fork. Prebake for 15–20 minutes.

✓ Meanwhile, in a dry bowl, beat egg whites with cream of tartar and salt until stiff peaks form. Incorporate the sugar. Reserve 1/3 cup beaten egg white for topping.

✓ Fold fruit into remaining egg white.

✓ Remove prebaked crust from oven and reduce temperature to 250°F. Spread toasted nut powder on bottom of pie crust. Fill with the egg-white-and-fruit mixture. Spread reserved whites on top. Bake in slow oven at least 1 hour.

Serves 6

1 pound red currants
1/2 cup hazelnuts, or coconut, ground finely
Pâte brisée for a 1-crust pie
7 egg whites
Pinch of cream of tartar
Pinch of salt
1 1/4 cups sugar

Serve warm or cold with a chilled dessert wine.

Flan Cake from Brittany
Far breton nature

The Morbihan department, on the southern coast of the Breton peninsula, is the only part of Brittany that does not bear a French name. Morbihan is its original name in the Breton language.
The far, a custardy flanlike cake—with its original name—has been prepared for centuries.
"The far is the dish most emblematic of Brittany. The preparation is simple, the ingredients are always at hand, and the result is excellent."

François Goulard
Deputy of Morbihan

✓ Preheat oven to 350°F.
✓ Butter a deep ovenproof dish with 1 teaspoon butter.
✓ In a bowl, mix flour, sugar, and salt. Stir in one egg at a time.
✓ Melt the remaining butter. Whisk it into the flour mixture, then whisk in milk and vanilla. Pour batter into buttered dish and bake 1 hour.
✓ Serve warm or cold.

Variation: This *far* can also be prepared with a layer of sliced apples on the bottom.

Serves 6
1 1/2 cups flour
2/3 cup sugar
Pinch of salt
5 eggs
4 tablespoons unsalted butter
2 1/2 cups milk
1 tablespoon vanilla extract

Monkfish Roasted in Bacon
Rôti de lotte groisillonne

"This traditional recipe from the island of Groix—one of Brittany's jewels, off Lorient harbor—showcases two of our leading local products: the noble and tasty monkfish, and pork, in its smoked form. Easy to prepare, this dish may be enjoyed with a dry white wine or a good Breton cider."

Françoise
Olivier-Coupeau
Deputy of Morbihan

Serves 6

1 2-pound monkfish tail, skinned, spine removed by fishmonger
1 garlic clove
2 slices pork slab, 1/2 inch thick
2 tablespoons Dijon mustard
10 slices bacon
Pepper
2 cups white wine
1 cup crème fraiche

✓ Preheat oven to 300°F.

✓ Stud fish with slivers of garlic. Spread mustard onto the 2 slices pork slab, and insert between halves of monkfish where the spine apparatus used to be. Wrap fish with bacon slices. Pepper (do not salt), and tie with kitchen twine, like a roast. Place in an ovenproof dish.

✓ Bake 10 minutes. Pull roast out and pour wine over it. Continue baking another 20 minutes. (Time will depend on thickness of fish. It is cooked when the flesh is tender—test by inserting fork.)

✓ Remove fish to a serving dish. Stir crème fraiche into wine. Pour over fish and serve.

Rice is a good accompaniment, or the pickled seaweed called salicornes.

Greengage Tart

Tarte aux mirabelles

"This tart is particularly good served warm. While it is often prepared with a migaine—*a mixture of eggs, milk, and cream—I prefer it simply with the fruit. Greengages from Lorraine ripen beginning in the second week of August, and are known for their golden color and their sweet juiciness.*

"Should you prefer a tarter flavor, use damson plums, the elongated purple ones, which are quite different from ordinary plums. Italian prune-plums, more easily found in America, are a fine substitute."

Denis Jacquat
Deputy of Moselle

✓ Preheat oven to 350°F.
✓ Roll out dough. Line a tart mold, crimping the border attractively. Prick dough all over with a fork.
✓ Sprinkle the bottom of the tart with breadcrumbs; these will absorb the fruit juices exuded in baking. Arrange the greengages, cut side up, in concentric circles, fitting them in snugly.
✓ Bake for 30–45 minutes, until the pastry is nicely browned and the fruit softened.
✓ Allow to cool slightly. Just before serving, sprinkle with sugar, vanilla-flavored or plain.

Serves 6

Puff pastry, or pâte brisée, for a 1-crust pie
1/4 cup breadcrumbs
1 1/2 pounds greengages, cut in half and pitted
1/4 cup sugar or vanilla sugar

The tarte aux mirabelles *can be enjoyed accompanied by champagne, or even coffee.*

Veal Paupiettes with Ham and Eggs
Nids d'hirondelles

The name nids d'hirondelles *here does not refer to the "swallow's nests" used in Chinese soup. In Lorraine they are paupiettes, rather like the ones called "veal birds" in English. In many homes, these egg-filled* nids d'hirondelles *are traditionally served at Easter. "This recipe, prepared exquisitely by my wife, was handed down to her by her grandmother, a native of Lorraine and a cordon bleu cook."*

Céleste Lett
Deputy of Moselle

Serves 6
6 large, thin veal slices
2 tablespoons Dijon mustard
6 slices ham
1 cup grated Gruyère cheese
6 hard-boiled eggs, peeled
2 tablespooons peanut oil
1 shallot, minced
1 tomato, quartered
1 carrot, peeled and sliced
1 bouquet garni
Pepper and salt
1 pound white mushrooms, sliced (optional)
2 tablespoons cognac
1 cup crème fraiche

✔ On each piece of veal, spread 1 teaspoon mustard, line with a slice of ham, sprinkle with grated cheese, and top with a hard-boiled egg. Wrap the meat around the egg to form a paupiette, and tie with kitchen twine.

✔ In a deep skillet, heat oil and sauté paupiettes with shallot until meat is browned on all sides. Add carrot, tomato, bouquet garni, pepper, and salt. If you have opted for mushrooms, add them as well. Pour in enough water to come halfway up the paupiettes. Cover and cook over low heat for 45 minutes.

✔ Remove paupiettes and, with a sharp (or electric) carving knife, cut each in two lengthwise. Discard strings and arrange the halves cut side up, for a presentation to please the eye and the palate.

✔ Taste sauce and adjust seasoning. Stir in cognac and crème fraiche. Pour sauce into a sauceboat and pass separately.

✔ Alsatian *spaetzel* or other noodles are recommended with the swallows' nests.

Pork Roast with Greengages

Rôti de porc aux mirabelles

The Moselle department, on the German border, is the part of Lorraine that changed hands most regularly, being annexed to Germany in 1871–1919 and again in 1940–1944 before returning to France for good. The cuisine, however, has always been a happy alliance of the two national influences. This recipe was provided by Marie-Jo Zimmermann, deputy of Moselle.

Serves 6

2–3 pounds boneless pork shoulder roast

Pepper and salt

1 cabbage, washed, outer leaves reserved

6 sage leaves

10 tablespoons lard

6 potatoes, peeled and halved

1 cup chicken stock

1/3 cup sugar

2 pounds greengages

✓ Preheat oven to 425°F.

✓ Season pork with salt and pepper. Envelop in outer cabbage leaves and tie with kitchen twine, tucking sage leaves underneath. In a roasting pan, put 2 tablespoons lard and the meat, and place in hot oven. Roast for 1 1/2 hours, reducing heat to 250°F after about 10 minutes, when meat begins to sizzle. Pour in a little water or stock, and baste now and then to ensure the roast won't become dry.

✓ Quarter cabbage lengthwise. Immerse in a kettle of boiling salted water and cook 10 minutes. Drain. Chop roughly.

✓ In a heavy casserole, heat remaining lard and stir cabbage for a few minutes until well coated. Add potatoes and stock. Cover and cook over low heat for 1 1/2 hours, checking seasoning after 1 hour.

✓ In a large saucepan, heat 1/3 cup sugar in 1 quart water until sugar dissolves. Add greengages, and cook 10 minutes. Drain. Reserve 1/4 cup syrup.

✓ When pork is done, remove from oven and let it rest 15 minutes, loosely covered. Place greengages in roasting pan and return to oven to simmer in roasting juices for several minutes, adding a bit of syrup if needed.

✓ Carve pork into slices. Top with a few greengages. Surround with cabbage and potato. Place remaining greengages in a bowl and pass separately.

Roasted Pike Perch with Potatoes Boulangère and Roasted Tomato

Sandre rôti sur peau, boulangère de pommes de terre et tomates confites

The Nièvre department is in the center of France, in Burgundy. The river Nièvre for which it is named is a minor waterway that flows, at the departmental capital Nevers, into the mighty Loire on whose Nivernais banks grow the Pouilly-Fuissé wines that would accompany this sandre to perfection.

"Rich, generous, and abundant in all aspects of agriculture, our Nièvre department also is home, in the sandy recesses of the Loire, to the noble sandre. This pike perch has a refined and tasty flesh that has inspired many a chef."

Martine Carrillon-Couvreur
Deputy of Nièvre

✔ For the *tomates confites*, preheat oven to 200°F. Plunge tomatoes in boiling water for 1 second. Refresh in ice water. Peel. Cut into quarters and remove seeds. Place on a baking sheet lined with parchment paper, season, and drizzle with olive oil. Bake 2 hours. Reserve, and reheat at serving time.

✔ For the *boulangère* of potatoes, preheat oven to 300°F.

✔ Cut the bacon into sticks about 1/4 inch square and 1/2 inch long. In a large, deep skillet, sauté bacon with onion for 10 minutes. Meanwhile, peel potatoes and cut into 1/8-inch slices (a mandoline is useful here). Add to skillet, moisten with chicken stock, and cook for 15 minutes.

✔ In a buttered baking dish, layer onion, bacon, and potato, interspersed with slices of butter. Bake 1 hour.

✔ In an overproof skillet, heat olive oil. Sauté fish, skin side down, until skin is crisp. Place skillet in oven to finish cooking, about 10 minutes. Do not turn fish over.

✔ On each serving plate, place a layer of potato *boulangère* in a circular design, topped by a filet of pike, and garnished with roasted tomato, a small goat cheese, and a sprig of chervil. Dot with salted butter all over, and serve.

Serves 4

4 filets of pike perch, each about 6 ounces
1–2 tablespoons olive oil
4 small goat cheeses
4 sprigs chervil
4 tablespoons salted butter

For the tomatoes:
2 tomatoes
Pepper and salt
Olive oil

For the potatoes:
1/2 pound onions, peeled and sliced
1/2 pound slab bacon
5 pounds potatoes
2 cups chicken stock
2 sticks salted butter

Beef Stew in Beer

Carbonade, frites et bière du Nord

"We have agreed to jointly offer this dish, a classic in the north of France and in Belgium, with which our Nord department shares a long border. Highly regarded in the gastronomy of the region for its exquisite and subtle sweet-sour flavors, the carbonade of beef is steeped in our local beer, which imparts a distinctive taste. Like all stews, this one benefits from resting and reheating. The carbonade is served either with steamed potatoes or, more often, with our famous frites, accompanied by some strong mustard and, of course, a good chti (Nord) beer."

Jean-Pierre Decool
Bernard Gérard
Deputies of Nord

✓ In a heavy-bottomed casserole, heat butter and brown meat on all sides. Add onions and cook until translucent. Add garlic, thyme, bay leaves, pepper, and salt. Turn heat to low, add beer and *pain d'épices*. Cover and cook at a bare simmer for at least 3 hours.

Note: The *pain d'épices* is a loaf cake made of two kinds of flour and such spices as ginger, cinnamon, aniseed, orange zest, and honey. An approximation in the United States might be gingerbread.

Serves 6

2 pounds stewing beef, cut in 2-inch pieces
1/2 pound onions, peeled and chopped
4 tablespoons butter
1 garlic clove
1 sprig thyme
2 bay leaves
Pepper and salt
1 1/2 cups dark beer
2 slices *pain d'épices*

Sugar Tart
Tarte au sucre

The tarte au sucre *is a traditional dessert also in Québec—not surprisingly, since the earliest explorers and settlers came largely from the coastal regions of the north of France. In French Canada maple sugar is sometimes substituted, but brown sugar or vergeoise is used invariably in the Nord department, where the cultivation of sugar beets is an important part of the economy.*
"A veritable delight!! You can serve the sugar tart with vanilla ice cream, or with a creamy custard sauce, perhaps mocha flavored."

Jean-Jacques Candelier
Deputy of Nord

Serves 6

2 tablespoons dry yeast
1/3 cup warm milk
1/2 pound flour
3 eggs
1/4 cup superfine white sugar
(you can obtain this by putting granulated sugar in a blender)
1/2 teaspoon fine salt
9 tablespoons butter
2/3 cup brown sugar
1 cup heavy cream

✓ In a small bowl, dilute yeast with a pinch of sugar and the warm milk. In a larger bowl, put the flour. Make a well in the center, break 1 egg in it, and add sugar, salt, yeast mixture, and 6 tablespoons cold butter, diced. Knead until it forms a smooth ball of dough. Cover. Let it rise for 3 hours.
✓ Preheat oven to 450°F.
✓ Punch down the dough, roll it out, and fit it into a high-sided round baking dish. Spread brown sugar evenly over the dough.
✓ In a bowl, whisk remaining 2 eggs, heavy cream, and remaining butter. Pour over brown sugar. Bake 25 minutes.
✓ Cool slightly before serving: hot sugar can burn.

Rhubarb Tart

Tarte à la rhubarbe et vergeoise

"This rhubarb tart brings back many memories! First, there is the image of my grandfather, the master of our garden, with his magical touch. I would go with him to pick rhubarb and keep the widest leaf, which I would turn into a parasol or an umbrella, depending on the weather. Then I see my grandmother, mistress of the kitchen, who always looked away like a silent accomplice when I stole a piece of dough, or a spoonful of cream. And the rhubarb itself, so acid when raw, yet so smooth and sweet later, served in her tart.
"I am continuing the tradition with my own grandchildren, who love the tart, and the rituals that go with it."

Françoise Hostalier
Deputy of the Nord

✓ Preheat oven to 350°F.

✓ Roll out dough and line a tart mold. Spread rhubarb pieces evenly over dough.

✓ In a bowl, whisk eggs, sugar, and crème fraiche. Pour over rhubarb, making sure the pieces are all coated. Sprinkle with a generous layer of brown sugar. Bake 30 minutes.

✓ If you wish a crunchy top, remove from oven when not quite done, and turn up the temperature or preheat the broiler. Dot the surface with butter evenly, and add another layer of brown sugar. Return to oven until a caramelized crust forms.

✓ Serve either warm or cold.

Serves 6

Pastry dough (pâte brisée) for an 11-inch tart
5 stalks rhubarb, diced
5 eggs
5 tablespoons sugar
5 tablespoons crème fraiche
3 tablespoons brown sugar
2 tablespoons butter

173

Micheline's Maroilles Tart
Flamiche au maroilles, façon Micheline

"Who is Micheline? Micheline is my mother-in-law, who gave me this recipe and who is a native of Maroilles. I am pleased to pay tribute to her."

Christine Marin
Deputy of Nord

Makes 2 tarts

2 tablespoons dry yeast

Pinch of sugar

2/3 cup warm milk

1 stick plus 1 tablespoon butter

2 1/4 cups flour

Pinch of salt

1 egg, plus 1 yolk

1/2 Maroilles cheese

1/2 cup heavy cream

✓ In a small bowl, dilute yeast with sugar and 1/3 cup warm milk. Let it become thick and bubbly.

✓ In the remaining 1/3 cup milk, heat 1 stick butter until dissolved. Cool to tepid. (If it is hot, it will cook the eggs.)

✓ In a large bowl, combine 1 1/4 cups flour, eggs, and salt, mixing with your hands. Gradually work in milk-butter mixture and yeast mixture. Add remaining 1 cup flour, and knead until it forms a smooth, elastic ball. Cover bowl, and let rise 1 hour in a warm place.

✓ Preheat oven to 400°F.

✓ Punch risen dough down. Butter two 11-inch tart molds. Divide dough, roll out, and line molds.

✓ Cut Maroilles into 1/8-inch slices. Distribute over dough, without overlapping. Sprinkle with cream.

✓ Bake 18–20 minutes. Serve while still hot.

Terrine of Mixed Meats

Potjevlesch

"This typical, traditional French Flemish dish from the Nord department can be served as a main course, accompanied by a salad of chicons, our famous endives, or by our famous frites."

Christian Vanneste
Deputy of Nord

✓ Preheat oven to 350°F.
✓ Bone the meats and cut up roughly.
✓ Lay half the fatback strips on the bottom of an ovenproof dish with a cover. Add the meats alternately, seasoning with pepper and salt as you go. Fill in the gaps with onions. Press down firmly. Lay thyme and bay leaves on top.
✓ Dilute gelatin with wine. Pour over meats. Add liquid as necessary so meat is just covered. Lay remaining fatback strips on top. Put the cover on.
✓ Bake 3 hours. Cool. Refrigerate.

Serve cold. A good chti *beer—from the Nord, that is—is recommended with this dish.*

Serves 6

Thighs, drumsticks, and wings of 1 chicken
Thighs and forelegs of 1 rabbit
3/4 pound veal breast
3/4 pound pork shoulder
1/2 pound pork fatback, in strips
Pepper and salt
3 onions, finely chopped
3 sprigs thyme
3 bay leaves
3 tablespoons gelatin
1 cup white wine, or gin

Steamed Duck
Canard col-vert à l'étouffée

North of Paris, the Oise department is within commuting range—its capital, Beauvais, is just fifty miles distant—and gaining population. Yet much of it retains its rural character, with a full range of agricultural activity. The river Oise, which wends south to the Seine through the forest of Compiègne, where the World War I armistice was signed, is navigable and an important contributer to Paris's water supply. This recipe was provided by Olivier Dassault, deputy of Oise.

<u>Serves 4</u>

1 whole duck
Pepper and salt
2 tablespoons olive oil
1 carrot, minced
1 onion, minced
1 shallot, minced
1 celery stalk, minced
1/4 cup cognac
6 cups chicken stock
1 bay leaf
1 sprig thyme
1 sprig rosemary
2 star anise
2 cardamom pods
1 garlic clove, minced
1 tablespoon potato starch or cornstarch

For the garnishes:

1 cup pearl onions
2 teaspoons sugar
Pepper and salt
1 Golden Delicious apple
2 tablespoons butter
1/2 pound chanterelles
1 shallot, finely chopped
1 tablespoon chives, finely chopped

✓ Preheat oven to 350°F.

✓ Rub duck with salt and pepper inside and out. Poke holes with a knife throughout. In a heavy kettle, heat olive oil. Lightly brown duck on all sides. Reserve on a holding platter. Remove most of accumulated fat from casserole.

✓ In remaining fat, sauté the *brunoise* of carrot, onion, shallot, and celery for 5 minutes. Pour in cognac. Ignite. When flames subside, add chicken stock, herbs, spices, and garlic. Return duck to casserole. Bring up to a simmer. Cover casserole and put in oven for 1 hour and 15 minutes.

✓ Remove duck and keep warm. On top of stove, skim stock to remove visible fat, then reduce stock by two-thirds. In a small bowl, dilute starch in cold water. Pour into casserole and stir until thickened. Pepper and salt to taste. Strain sauce through a sieve and place in a sauceboat. Keep warm.

✓ Prepare the garnishes: In a small saucepan, place pearl onions in boiling water with 1 teaspoon sugar and pepper and salt, cook 15 minutes, and drain. Peel and slice the apple, and cook in a nonstick pan with 1 tablespoon butter and 1 teaspoon sugar. In a skillet, heat remaining 1 tablespoon butter and sauté chanterelles, shallot, and chives 2 minutes.

✓ Carve the duck: Cut off legs and wings, bone out the breast, and place in serving pieces on platter. Pour sauce over duck. Surround with vegetables. Serve.

Tarte Tatin of Endives, Bacon, and Cheese
Tatin d'endives au rollot

"The Rollot is a specialty of our region, Picardy, a round or heart-shaped soft cow's-milk cheese with a washed rind. When Louis XIV was traveling in Picardy and tasted the Rollot, he was so enchanted that he declared it a royal cheese and ordered it for the court at Versailles. Since that time, the Rollot has again become popular and is being sold throughout the country. We are also the second largest producers in France of that exquisite but sometimes underappreciated vegetable, the endive."

François-Michel Gonnot
Jean-François Mancel
Deputies of Oise

Serves 4

2 pounds Belgian endives, trimmed and washed
1/4 cup canola oil
1/2 cup light brown sugar
6 ounces bacon cubes (lardons)
4 tablespoons butter
1/2 cup flour
1/2 pound Rollot cheese, rind removed
1 1/3 cups 2-percent milk
4 tablespoons hazelnuts, crushed
1 tablespoon crème fraiche
1/2 teaspoon grated nutmeg
Pepper and salt
Pastry dough (pâte brisée) for a 1-crust pie

✓ Cut endives in four, lengthwise. In a skillet, heat oil and sauté endives until they turn translucent. Sprinkle with brown sugar and cook a few minutes to caramelize them. Remove endives to absorbent paper. Reserve.

✓ In the same skillet, sauté lardons 5 minutes. Reserve.

✓ Preheat oven to 425°F.

✓ In a saucepan, melt butter, stir in flour, and allow to cook in briefly. Cut Rollot into small cubes and add along with milk, hazelnuts, crème fraiche, nutmeg, salt, and pepper. Stir and simmer 5 minutes.

✓ In a tart mold, arrange endive wedges in a starburst pattern. Sprinkle lardons over endives. Add contents of skillet.

✓ Roll out dough into a circle 2 inches larger than the mold. Place over filling, tucking dough in thoroughly all around the inside of the mold. Bake 25–30 minutes or until crust is golden.

✓ As soon as it comes out of the oven, invert a platter over the tart and flip to turn it out. If any pieces stick to the mold, pry them loose with a spatula and fit them back into the tart filling.

✓ Serve warm.

Marinated Camembert with Pear-Apple Chutney

Camembert mariné au poiré Domfront, chutney aux poires et pommes

In Normandy, Camembert is made of raw cow's milk, but for export the milk is pasteurized, which lessens a little its unique flavor. The rind of the authentic Camembert de Normandie is lightly rust-tinged, not chalk white.

"Jewel of Normandy, the Camembert cheese is savored the world over. Natives frequently enjoy their Camembert with a glass of poiré—a drink little known outside Normandy because of its limited local production. With its amber color and sweet pear flavor, but strong and effervescent, poiré ("perry" in England) is similar to apple hard cider. In a spirit of regional pride, locals have 'married' their Camembert to their poiré. In my view, everything about the Camembert makes one appreciate the tranquil charm of a true countryside where living is still sweet."

Jean-Claude Lenoir
Deputy of Orne

✓ Cut Camembert in four without separating the pieces. In a flat bowl, put cheese, add pear cider to cover, top with a lid, and refrigerate 24 hours.

✓ Peel, core, and chop apples and pears. Place in a saucepan with remaining chutney ingredients. Heat to a high bubble, and cook until mixture turns syrupy. Fruit should remain discrete but tender. Cool.

✓ Remove Camembert from poiré. Drain and slice thinly. Place slices on a platter and top each with a teaspoon of the chutney. Serve with more poiré.

For the chutney:
1 Camembert cheese
1 bottle poiré
For the chutney:
2 Gala apples
2 Bartlett pears
2 cups sugar
1 cup raisins
1 cup cider vinegar
1 cup balsamic vinegar
2 cloves
1 cinnamon stick
1/4 teaspoon ground ginger
Pinch of cayenne pepper
Salt

Boulogne Fisherman's Chowder

Caudière à la boulonnaise—le vrai plat des pêcheurs boulonnais!

Named for the narrow passage of water that links the English Channel and the North Sea, Pas-de-Calais is France's next-to-northernmost department. During World War II, Pas-de-Calais became the target of Operation Fortitude, the Allies' plan to deceive the Germans into believing that the D-day invasion of Europe was to take place there rather than in Normandy.

"Being a native of Boulogne-sur-Mer, France's premier fishing harbor and the principal European center for the processing of fish and seafood, I find myself automatically drawn to products of the sea. If my gustatory tendencies incline to the celebrated herring en papillote or the traditional sole meunière, my favorite dish remains our Caudière à la Boulonnaise, the hearty stew that nourished my childhood."

Frédéric Cuvillier
Deputy of Pas-de-Calais

✓ Make sure the fish are well cleaned. Slice the cod thickly. Remove heads and tails of mackerel and whiting and cut crosswise into generous chunks. Scrub and beard the mussels.

✓ In a large kettle, heat oil and butter. Sauté onion and leek gently until cleared. Add carrots, garlic, and bouquet garni, and cook 5 minutes more. Add potatoes, pepper and salt, and 12 cups hot water. Cook at a simmer for a further 15 minutes.

✓ Now add all the fish, and the mussels. By the time the pot comes back to a boil, the cooking of the fish will be almost complete. Continue to cook for about 3 minutes, or until the mussels are open.

✓ Working gently, remove fish and mussels to a serving platter, surrounded by vegetables. Serve the broth separately.

✓ Accompany with croutons, and with a white beer or a dry Graves.

Serves 6–8
2 pounds cod
2 mackerel
2 whiting
1 1/2 pounds mussels
2 tablespoons olive oil
2 tablespoons butter
2 onions, finely chopped
3 leeks, well washed and finely chopped
3 carrots, peeled and thinly sliced
3 garlic cloves, smashed
1 bouquet garni
2 pounds potatoes, peeled and thinly sliced
Pepper and salt

Kermesse Custard Tart

Tarte à gros bords, ou Tarte à papin, ou Tarte de Ducasse

The ducasse, *a yearly celebration in the north of France and Belgium, started in the Middle Ages as a patron-saint festival (*ducasse *comes from* dédicace*) in the town of Ath in Hainaut. The fair goes on for several days, with many pageants, and much feasting. The traditional* tarte à papin *specific to Pas-de-Calais is a pie of brioche dough with sides higher than most, filled with a vanilla-milk cream—the* papin *or* libouli *(*lait bouilli*).*
"This is our family recipe, the one my grandmother made. Traditionally the tart was cooked in the village baker's oven, in great numbers, during the ducasse *celebrations—or for family reunions, or for large banquets."*

Daniel Fasquelle
Deputy of Pas-de-Calais

<u>Makes 2 tarts, each serving 8.</u>
Recipe may be halved.
For the crust:
2 tablespoons dry yeast
1 teaspoon sugar
2 cups flour
Pinch of sugar
Pinch of salt
8 tablespoons butter
3/4 cup warm milk
1 egg plus 1 yolk
For the cream:
2 whole eggs plus 4 yolks
1 1/2 cups flour
8 cups milk
2 tablespoons vanilla extract
1 cup pitted prunes (optional)
1 whole egg, beaten with
2 tablespoons strong,
cold coffee

✓ In a small bowl, dilute yeast with a little warm water and the sugar. Allow it to proof (become creamy and bubbly) for a few minutes.
✓ In a large bowl, combine flour with a pinch of sugar and salt. Make a well in the center.
✓ In a saucepan, heat butter in milk until melted. In a small bowl, whisk eggs. Pour into the flour well the warm milk and butter, eggs, and yeast. Knead to form a smooth ball of dough. Let it rest for 15 minutes.
✓ Roll out, and line pie mold, building up dough on sides to make a thick and high rim. Let it rest another 15 minutes, while you make the *papin*.
✓ Preheat oven to 400°F.
✓ In a bowl, whisk eggs. Add flour and 2 cups cold milk. Stir well.
✓ In a large saucepan, bring 6 cups milk to a boil with the sugar and vanilla. Turn heat off and incorporate by whisking egg/flour mixture.
✓ Bring to a boil again, stirring for a minute or two, then remove from heat. Repeat.
✓ When cream has cooled, spread into crust. Prunes may be added if wished. Lastly, brush cream filling with egg-coffee wash.
✓ Bake 30–45 minutes. Serve.

Rabbit Stewed in Wine

Lapin en civet

"I have been cooking this particular rabbit stew for the past forty years. On the farms of the Auvergne, the domestic rabbit was, along with chicken, the Sunday complement to the daily fare of our farm-raised pork— killed in great solemnity each year during the fête du cochon. *Of my culinary repertory, and despite my duties as deputy, this recipe remains the one I still like to prepare, however rarely.*

"This rabbit dish reminds me of my paternal grandfather, a peillarot— *gatherer of rabbit pelts. He would ride his bicycle from farm to farm, enjoy some wine with each farmer, buy the rabbit skins, and then watch the children scramble to collect the few yellow coins from the sale. After these stops, Grandfather would ride back home, rather less steady than when he started, skins hanging from the back and front of his bicycle."*

André Chassaigne
Deputy of Puy-de-Dôme

Serves 6

1–2 rabbits, about 4–5 pounds each
3 tablespoons flour
1/2 pound thick bacon, cut up in lardons
1 tablespoon olive oil
4 shallots, finely chopped
4 carrots, peeled and diced
1 bottle red wine, preferably from Auvergne
1 bouquet garni
Pepper and salt
1/4 teaspoon grated nutmeg
20 pearl onions

✔ Cut up the rabbit in serving pieces—or have the butcher do it—making sure there are no small shards of bone. Coat rabbit pieces in flour.

✔ In a heavy casserole, over moderate heat, sauté lardons until translucent. Reserve. Add oil to fat from lardons and brown rabbit on all sides. Stir in shallots and carrots. Let them brown a few minutes as well.

✔ Pour in wine, adding a little water if need be to cover meat. Add lardons, bouquet garni, pepper, salt, and nutmeg. Cover and simmer 1 hour. Taste and adjust seasoning. Add pearl onions. Continue simmering.

✔ Recommendation: At serving time, we, in Auvergne, dilute one cup pork blood with a few spoonfuls of sauce. Off heat, stir blood into the pot. Do not allow to boil.

✔ (In the absence of blood, use 2 squares of unsweetened dark chocolate to give the sauce its substance and dark color.)

✔ Serve with boiled potatoes.

Apple in Puff Pastry

La pompe aux pommes

*Situated in the Auvergne region in south-central France, the Puy-de-Dôme department takes its name from a dome of lava that erupted centuries ago from the youngest volcano in the Massif Central. **Puy** is the geological term used locally for volcanic hill or crater. Although the department is largely mountainous, the broad central valley of the Allier supports varied agriculture including the raising of livestock, grains—and fruits. This recipe was provided by Louis Giscard d'Estaing, deputy of Puy-de-Dôme*

Serves 4

4–5 pounds apples
1/2 cup sugar
1/2 teaspoon cinnamon
2 sheets puff pastry
1 egg yolk

✓ Preheat oven to 400°F.
✓ Peel, core, and dice the apples. In a bowl, mix apples, sugar, and cinnamon.
✓ Roll out 2 puff pastry rectangles. Spread apples to cover one rectangle, leaving a 1-inch border. Moisten the border of the dough. Place second puff pastry rectangle over apples. Seal by pinching the edges tightly.
✓ In a small bowl, beat yolk with a tablespoon of water. With a pastry brush, paint egg over dough.
✓ Bake 45 minutes. Serve.

Basque Scrambled Eggs with Peppers and Tomatoes
Pipérade

The Pyrénées-Atlantiques, the southwesternmost department of France, is Basque country, and **pipérade** *is one of the Basque country's signature dishes. It can be served at breakfast or lunch or, with or without egg, as an accompaniment to grilled meat or to fish freshly caught in the Atlantic off the seaside resorts of Biarritz and Saint-Jean-de-Luz. This recipe was provided by Jean Lassalle, deputy of Pyrénées-Atlantiques.*

✔ In a heavy saucepan, heat 2 tablespoons olive oil and cook garlic until golden. Add onion, bouquet garni, and rind or ham bone. Cover and cook over low heat for 30 minutes.

✔ In a skillet, heat remaining 2 tablespoons olive oil and cook peppers gently for 15 minutes.

✔ Transfer peppers to saucepan and stir in tomatoes, tomato paste, wine, and 1 cup water. Cook covered for 30 minutes over low heat.

✔ Remove ham bone and bouquet garni. Check sauce and add salt if needed. Season to taste with pepper, sugar, and piment d'Espelette.

✔ In a large pan, heat butter and scramble eggs, adding some of the Basquaise sauce from the saucepan. Meanwhile, sauté ham slices separately.

✔ Serve a ham slice and a mound of pipérade on each plate, sprinkled with parsley. Pass the remaining Basquaise sauce in a bowl.

Serves 4

4 tablespoons olive oil
1 pound onions, finely chopped
4 garlic cloves, minced
1 bouquet garni
1 rind or bone of country ham, or ham hock
1/2 pound bell peppers, seeds and stem removed, quartered
2 pounds tomatoes, peeled, seeded, and chopped
1/4 cup tomato paste
1 cup Jurançon or other dry white wine
Pepper and salt
1 pinch sugar
1 pinch piment d'Espelette or, if unavailable, hot paprika
3 tablespoons butter
8 eggs, lightly beaten
4 slices Bayonne, or Serrano ham, or prosciutto
2 tablespoons parsley, finely chopped

Pyrenean Potage with Duck Confit

Garbure bigourdane

"This recipe is a specialty of our department (along with the conifer-shaped cake called Rocher des Pyrénées or gâteau à la broche). In its simplified version, without meat, the soup was daily fare for many, from a long time ago when the center of our high Pyrénées country was the independent county of Bigorre. In the fifteenth century Bigorre joined with Béarn to the west, and the dish is now also known as garbure béarnaise."

Pierre Forgues
Deputy of Hautes-Pyrénées

Serves 6

1/2 pound pork fatback
1 shank of pork (optional, see note)
2 carrots, thickly sliced
2 leeks, trimmed, cut in 1-inch lengths
2 onions, quartered
2 turnips, in large cubes
2 garlic cloves
1 large bouquet garni
Pepper and salt
4 potatoes, in large cubes
1 cup cooked white beans
1 small Savoy cabbage, cut into 6 wedges
3 duck thighs or 6 drumsticks, confit (see note)

✓ In a kettle, put fatback, shank (if using), carrots, leeks, onions, turnips, garlic, bouquet garni, pepper, and salt. Cover with water and simmer for 1 1/4 hours.
✓ Add potatoes, beans, and cabbage. Top up water as needed. Continue simmering 55 minutes more. Adjust seasoning.
✓ Add duck pieces (if using), together with a bit of the fat in which they were preserved. Cook 10 more minutes. Serve.

Note: Use pork if duck is not available. But whole duck legs are increasingly found already *confit* (slow-cooked and preserved in their own fat) in good supermarkets. Or they may be mail-ordered at dartagnan.com or bellabellagourmet.com or other online suppliers.

Partridge with Seville Oranges in Sauce

Perdreau à la sauce catalane

As its name proclaims, the department of Pyrénées-Orientales is located at the eastern (Mediterranean) end of France's mountainous border with Spain. Its coastal area around Perpignan, called the Roussillon, is directly north of Catalonia and the Costa Brava, and the cross-border neighbors share both linguistic and culinary influences.

"A traditional Catalan dish particularly popular in the Roussillon, copied (and amplified) from a little notebook of recipes written by my grandfather, almost a century ago, titled Recettes culinaires simples (cuisine roussillonnaise traditionnelle—1925)."

François Calvet
Deputy of Pyrénées-Orientales

✔ Cut up the partridges (or have your butcher do it): Halve each bird through the breastbone, and cut out and discard the backbone. If you like, cut each half in half again, trying not to splinter the ribs.

✔ In a large casserole or Dutch oven, heat olive oil. Brown the partridge pieces. Reserve.

✔ Add onion and 1 garlic clove, minced. When browned, stir in the flour and cook 3 more minutes. Stir in 2 cups water, the tomato purée, pepper and salt, and the remaining garlic cloves, whole. Return partridge pieces to the pot. Cook gently for about 1 hour, adding water if needed.

✔ Blanch the oranges to reduce the bitterness of their skin. Cut into slices and add to sauce for last 15–20 minutes. Serve.

This recipe can also be prepared with pork tenderloin, or with pigeon.

Serves 4

2 partridges, about 1 pound each
2 tablespoons olive oil
1 onion, finely chopped
5 garlic cloves
1 tablespoon flour
2 cups tomato purée
Pepper and salt
2 bitter (Seville) oranges

Catalan Meatballs with Olives in Tomato Sauce
Boles de picoulat

"Boles de picoulat—the very sound of its name has a way of opening my appetite. These typically Catalan meatballs in a sauce with olives bring back the happy times of childhood. A winter dish, it is equally welcome in summer. Served as the whole meal, boles de picoulat *used to be considered the food of the poor, yet it remains rich not only in calories but in conviviality."*

Daniel Mach
Deputy of Pyrénées-Orientales

Makes about 28 meatballs, serving 6–7

1 pound ground beef
1 pound pork sausage meat
2 slices day-old bread, soaked in milk and squeezed dry
3 eggs
2 onions, finely chopped
Pepper and salt
1/4 cup flour
1/4 cup olive oil
1 16-ounce can crushed tomatoes
1/4 cup tomato paste
1 cup olives, green or black
1 cup white mushrooms, sliced

✔ In a bowl, combine the two meats, soaked bread, eggs, 1 chopped onion, pepper, and salt. Mix thoroughly. Form balls, about the size of an apricot.
✔ Place flour in a small bowl. Roll meatballs in flour. Reserve on paper towel.
✔ In a skillet, heat olive oil. Fry meatballs until browned all over. Drain on paper towel.
✔ In a heavy casserole, heat 1 tablespoon oil and fry remaining onion. Stir in flour and, after a minute, 1 cup warm water to thicken, then the tomatoes, tomato paste, pepper and salt, and another 1–2 cups water. Simmer 10 minutes. Add meatballs, olives, and mushrooms. Let simmer for 1 hour. Watch level of liquid, and add water if necessary, but the sauce should be a bit thick. Adjust seasoning and serve.

"This dish is traditionally accompanied by white beans. The recommended wine would be a Côte-du-Roussillon Villages, aged in oak. A good first course might be an escalivade (mixed roasted vegetables in oil) with white anchovies, and a Catalan conclusion for the meal could be a flan, with a glass of Muscat de Rivesaltes."

Sweet Yeast Dumplings

Pains soufflés à la vapeur (Dampfnüdle)

"Here is a typical Alsatian recipe that I particularly appreciate because I happen to be fond of yeast dough. In Alsace, dampfnüdle are often an entire supper."

Émile Blessig
Deputy of Bas-Rhin

Serves 5–6

2 tablespoons dry yeast
1 cup warm milk
1 teaspoon sugar
4 tablespoons butter, softened
Pinch of salt
2 1/2 cups flour, plus more for rolling out
2 eggs
1/3 cup oil

✓ In a bowl, dilute yeast with milk and sugar. When mixture becomes a little foamy, add softened butter, salt, sifted flour, and eggs. Knead the dough, lifting it and incorporating some air, until it becomes smooth, holds together, and is no longer sticky.

✓ Cover bowl with a towel and set in a warm place. Allow dough to rise 1 hour or until doubled in size.

✓ On a floured work surface, punch dough down and roll it out with a floured rolling pin, leaving it 1-inch thick. With a glass dipped in flour, cut out circles of dough about 2 inches in diameter. Place circles on a sheet. Cover and let them rise 30 minutes.

✓ In a Dutch oven or a heavy kettle with a close-fitting cover, heat oil.

✓ When it is hot, add rounds of dough, leaving space for them to expand. Quickly pour in 1 cup warm water and close the lid immediately. Cook for 10 minutes. Remove lid, lift dumplings with tongs onto a platter, and keep warm.

✓ Cook remaining batches in the same manner.

"The dampfnüdle are ready when a golden crust is beginning to form. Serve with a compote of stewed fruit, fresh or dried, or with fruit canned in syrup—but in any case make sure there is plenty of sweet juice."

Alsatian Stuffed Pasta Rolls

Tranches farcies et roulées (Fleischschnaka)

Charming Strasbourg, the seat of the European Parliament and the Council of Europe, is truly international, and half the population of the Lower Rhine department lives there. But the rest of the Bas-Rhin remains solidly Alsatian. As it borders Germany on both the north and the east, it reflects the strong culinary impact of its neighbor. A good example is the fleischschnacka, *with its* fleisch *(meat) filling and its* schnacka *(dialect for* Schnecke, *snail) shape. This recipe was provided by Jean-Philippe Maurer, deputy of Bas-Rhin.*

Serves 4

2/3 pound leftover cooked meats
1 onion, minced
1 garlic clove, minced
1/2 cup parsley, finely chopped
Pepper and salt
1/2 cup flour
3 tablespoons butter
1 cup olive oil
2 cups chicken stock

For the pasta dough:

3 eggs
1 tablespoon wine vinegar
1 tablespoon salt
1 tablespoon water
2 cups flour

✓ First make the pasta dough. In a bowl, combine eggs, vinegar, salt, and water, then add flour and knead until you obtain a smooth dough. This can be done in the food processor as well. Set dough aside for 30 minutes, covered with a damp cloth.

✓ Finely chop all meats, mix well with onion, garlic, and parsley, and season to taste.

✓ Roll out dough into a rectangle about 1/8 inch thick. Spread meat filling over the dough, leaving an empty border on one of the long edges. Beginning at the other long side, roll up the stuffed rectangle, jellyroll fashion, to form a long tube. Moisten the empty border with warm water and press well to seal.

✓ With a sharp knife, cut tube into slices 1–2 inches thick. Spread flour in a soup plate. Coat each slice with flour.

✓ In a skillet, heat olive oil and butter. Fry slices until golden on both sides. Pour chicken stock over slices, bring to a simmer, and cook 20 minutes.

Serve with a green salad.

Sweet Kougelhopf from Alsace

Kougelhopf sucré d'Alsace

"Choosing a representative recipe is not easy, for Alsatian cuisine is very rich, in all senses of the term. It not only offers the bounties of our terroir, *it also borrows entire chapters from our German cousins, especially in the area of charcuterie. But in the end I chose the kougelhopf.*

"A sort of brioche, the kougelhopf *(pronounced 'koogloff') seems to punctuate our deputies' daily schedules. No function, big or small, takes place without a slice of kougelhopf being offered, whether to elected members or citizens. No time for lunch? A slice or two of kougelhopf will do. It is even called 'the deputy's steak.'*

"There are several kinds of kougelhopf. I prefer the traditional sweet one, stuffed with raisins or currants, decorated with almonds, and sprinkled with confectioners' sugar. It goes well with a dry Alsatian wine, or a Muscat. The salted version, most often enjoyed with a glass of Gewurztraminer, of course has no powdered sugar or almonds, but it has walnuts inside and out, and bits of bacon replacing the raisins.

"Because Alsatian bakeries are closed on Sunday and there is no fresh bread, the kougelhopf lends a festive presence to the Sunday breakfast table.

"A word about the terracotta molds. Back in the twelfth century, the emperor Barbarossa accorded the potters of Soufflenheim the right in perpetuity to take clay out of the ground for their superbly decorated pottery. To cure one of the pretty kougelhopf molds, first immerse the pot in cold water for a few minutes, then dry it, butter it, bake it in a hot oven, and let it cool. Repeat the operation before placing the pot in service. No need to wash it after each use, merely wipe with a cloth."

Antoine Herth
Deputy of Bas-Rhin

✓ In a bowl, soak raisins in warm water (and a bit of rum, if you like).

✓ In another bowl, dilute yeast in 1/2 cup warm milk (not hot; it would kill the yeast) and mix in 3 tablespoons flour to make a small dough. Cover and leave to rise until double in size, about 30 minutes.

✓ In a larger bowl, mix remaining flour with sugar, salt, eggs, and remaining milk. Knead for 15 minutes to aerate the dough well. Incorporate softened butter.

✓ Add the risen "sponge" and knead until the dough is uniform, smooth, and detaches itself from the bowl. Cover and let rise in a warm place away from drafts for 1 hour.

✓ Punch down the dough. Add soaked raisins and mix to distribute evenly.

✓ Butter all the Bundt pan's ridges and depressions. Drop one almond in the bottom of each section. Put dough in mold, surrounding the chimney. Let rise again, covered and away from drafts, for at least 1 hour.

✓ Preheat oven to 400°F.

✓ When dough has risen to border of mold, place in oven on middle rack. Bake 50–55 minutes. If the top darkens too fast, cover with parchment paper.

✓ Turn mold upside down onto a cooling rack and unmold cake. Using a sieve, sprinkle with confectioners' sugar. Serve.

Serves 12, made in a 10-inch Bundt pan.

3/4 cup raisins
2 tablespoons dry yeast
1 cup warm milk
3 cups flour
1/3 cup sugar
1 tablespoon salt
2 eggs
10 tablespoons butter, softened
1/4 cup blanched almonds
1/2 cup confectioners' sugar

Choucroute Garnie
Choucroute

"The word choucroute *comes from the Alsatian* sûrkrut, *sour herb. It arrived in France before the Revolution with the Swiss Guard of the ancien régime. At that time the dish merely consisted of cabbage. By the nineteenth century, potatoes were added. When various meats and charcuterie appeared with it, it became* choucroute garnie.*
"Krautergersheim, south of Strasbourg, is the capital of cabbage for choucroute. This white cabbage is finely shredded, salted, and cured in barrels for several weeks. Choucroute* nouvelle *is made from* choux précoces, *cabbages that grow in just 90 days rather than 150, and are picked only between July 14 and November 15. This specialty is tender, sweet, and slightly sour, with only two weeks of fermentation. Recommended potatoes for choucroute are the variety called Charlotte. In America, Yukon gold might be a good equivalent.
"There's a plethora of choucroutes—the Choucroute Paysanne, Choucroute Strasbourgeoise, Choucroute Royale, Vigneronne, and many more—but the one I propose here is the traditional recipe."*

François Loos
Deputy of Bas-Rhin

Serves 8

5 pounds raw sauerkraut
3 garlic cloves, germ removed
2 cloves
1 or 2 sprigs thyme
1 bay leaf
6 juniper berries
12 peppercorns
1/2 pound goose or duck fat
2 onions, finely chopped
1 picnic ham
1 salted pork hock
1 pound slab bacon
1 bottle Riesling wine (or beer, or Crémant d'Alsace)
1 pound kielbasa
8 knockwurst
8–10 potatoes

✓ In a colander, run tepid water over sauerkraut for 5 minutes. Drain well, fluff with your fingers, and place briefly on a clean towel.

✓ Preheat oven to 350°F.

✓ In a piece of cheesecloth, assemble garlic, cloves, thyme, bay leaf, juniper berries, and peppercorns. Gather into a pouch and tie with kitchen twine.

✓ In a heavy ovenproof casserole, melt goose or duck fat and sauté onion until translucent. Add ham, pork hock, bacon, and cheesecloth pouch, and cover with sauerkraut. Season lightly. Pour in wine and enough water just to cover. Bring to a boil, reduce heat, place a sheet of parchment paper on top, and cover with lid. Place in oven, and bake for 1 1/2 hours.

✓ Toward the end of the baking time, boil the potatoes. Drain. Keep warm.

✓ In a kettle of simmering water, cook sausages for 15 minutes. Drain.

✓ Remove casserole from oven. Place meats on a carving board. Cut sausages and meats into serving pieces.

✓ On a platter, place sauerkraut in the center, with potatoes and all meats around it. Serve hot, passing Dijon mustard as condiment.

Alsatian One-Pot Baked Dinner

Bäckeoffe

"This recipe from my region takes its name from the way it is cooked. The bäckeoffe was prepared every Monday—washday—traditionally in a large oval earthenware terrine with a cover, and brought to the village baker's oven (bàchoofa in Alsatian) to be cooked there while the village ladies tended to the laundry, together. A very simple-to-make dish, I highly recommend it for an evening with friends or family. But while it takes little work, it does take time, so remember to do the marinating the day before."

Arlette Grosskost
Deputy of Haut-Rhin

✓ The day before, combine marinade ingredients in a bowl with pork, beef, lamb, pig's feet and tails. Mix well. Put into a plastic bag, well sealed. Refrigerate 24 hours.

✓ Mix dough ingredients, in a bowl or the food processor, to form a firm ball. Wrap in film. Reserve in the refrigerator.

✓ On cooking day, thinly slice the 3 onions and the potatoes.

✓ With a slotted spoon, remove vegetables and meats from marinade.

✓ In a skillet, melt lard. Sauté vegetables and onions from marinade. (If you wish, also sauté meats for deeper flavor, though this is not traditional.)

✓ In an earthenware casserole, put a good layer of potatoes, then the meats and sautéed vegetables, then a layer of sliced onions, the rest of the potatoes, and the rest of the onions. Pour in the wine from the marinade, add salt and enough stock to come halfway up the casserole.

✓ Preheat oven to 350°F.

✓ Roll out dough into a long ribbon. Lay it on the rim of the casserole. Tightly press casserole lid and seal with the ribbon of dough.

✓ Bake 2 1/2 or 3 hours. Serve with a good Alsatian wine.

Serves 6

1 pound pork loin, cubed
1 pound boneless beef shank, cubed
1 pound boneless lamb shoulder, cubed
2 pig's feet, split
2 pig's tails (optional)
3 onions
4 pounds potatoes
3 tablespoons lard or shortening
2 cups beef stock

For the marinade:

1 bottle white Alsatian wine (Riesling, Sylvaner)
1 bouquet garni
1 bay leaf
10 juniper berries
1 sprig thyme
1 onion, studded with 4 cloves
1 onion, sliced
2 leeks, trimmed and chopped
1 celery stalk, peeled and chopped
2 carrots, peeled and chopped
Pepper and salt

For the ribbon of dough:

1 cup flour
1 tablespoon shortening
1/3 cup ice water
1/4 teaspoon salt

Crisp-Fried Marinated Carp
Carpe frite sundgauvienne

"The seductive little area of the Sundgau, tucked between the valley of the Rhine, the Swiss border, and the Alsatian basin, is bucolic and restful—and a treat for gourmands. In the ponds of this valley, in medieval times, monks raised carp, which were cooked in a unique and delicious manner. This recipe, transmitted from generation to generation, is today one of the mainstays of Sundgau restaurants."

Jean-Luc Reitzer
Deputy of Haut-Rhin

Serves 4
3 pounds center-cut carp filets
1–2 cups white wine
Pepper and salt
1/2 cup fine semolina
Oil for frying

✓ If beginning with whole fish, choose 2 three-year-old carp, about 4 pounds each. From these, cut (or have your fishmonger cut) uniform *darnes*, or filet sections, 1/2 inch thick.

✓ In a flat-bottomed dish, put carp pieces. Pour in wine to cover, and marinate for 20 minutes.

✓ Remove fish from wine, drain, season with pepper and salt, and dredge in semolina.

✓ The fish will be fried in two stages. In a deep-fryer or a deep pan, heat at least 2 inches oil until moderately hot, about 330°F. Fry carp until golden outside, about 4–5 minutes. Remove and allow to cool for 10 minutes—or until you are ready to serve the meal.

✓ Increase oil heat to 365°F, and fry carp a second time, 3–4 minutes.

✓ Serve it with steamed potatoes or frites, a green salad, lemon wedges, and some mayonnaise. The fish is eaten with the fingers.

✓ A nice Alsatian white wine is recommended, such as a pinot blanc or Riesling.

Pâté in a Puff Pastry Crust

Pâté vigneron en croûte

"This recipe perfectly combines our native products with the art of gastronomic refinement. As one carves through the crust of the pâté, Alsace in all its subtlety seems to emerge in the harmonious alliance of aromas and flavors."

Éric Straumann
Deputy of Haut-Rhin

✔ Cut the pork and the veal into fine strips. Finely chop the onion and the parsley.

✔ In a bowl, combine and mix meats, onion, parsley, thyme, bay leaf, wine, cognac, salt, and pepper. Cover. Refrigerate overnight.

✔ Preheat oven to 300°F.

✔ Remove meats and onion from the marinade. Discard bay leaf and thyme.

✔ Roll out puff pastry into 2 rectangles, one to serve as the base, the other as the cover. In the cover rectangle, cut out 2 holes for chimneys, pinching the edges to create tiny "walls" so steam can escape without destroying the crust.

✔ On the base rectangle, pile the meat mixture, leaving an inch or so of border. Place the cover rectangle on top, sealing by pinching the two pastry sheets tightly all around.

✔ Beat egg with 1 tablespoon water. With a pastry brush, paint pastry cover and border with egg wash.

✔ Bake 50 minutes.

✔ Enjoy the pâté warm, with a green salad.

Serves 6

1 1/2 pounds pork shoulder
1/2 pound veal shoulder or boneless neck meat
1 onion
1/4 cup parsley
1 sprig thyme
1 bay leaf
3/4 cup Alsatian white wine
2 tablespoons cognac
1 teaspoon kosher salt
Pepper
2 pounds puff pastry
1 egg

Cardoons with Marrow
Cardon

The Rhône department in east-central France flanks the great waterway where it emerges from the Alps and turns south to form the riverine backbone of Provence. At that bend is Lyons, the regional capital and, in the eyes of many, the capital of French cuisine. Here are the temples of gastronomy of Paul Bocuse and disciples, where haute cuisine is paired with the great wines of the Côte Rôtie and Condrieu from the south of the Rhône department. Here too are the delightful bouchons, where bistro food is invariably washed down by a pot of Beaujolais grown just to the north.

"If there is a refined and delicious vegetable that the Lyonnais have made their own, it is the cardoon—a relative of the artichoke, though it grows in heads like celery. Little found elsewhere, it flourishes in the fields around Lyons and in the South of France. Prepared fresh, and served with all manner of meat juices, the stalks of the cardoon become incomparable when combined with poached beef marrow."

Jean-Louis Touraine
Deputy of Rhône

Serves 4

3 pounds cardoon stalks
Juice of 1 lemon
1 1/2 cups meat juice from beef or veal roast
1/2 pound marrow extracted from beef bones
Pepper and salt

✓ Peel cardoons, cut into 2-inch pieces, and soak in lemon water for 30 minutes.

✓ In a kettle, bring water to a boil. Cook cardoons for 30 minutes. Drain.

✓ In a skillet, heat meat juices. (If they are insufficient, make up the quantity with diluted *glace de viande*, meat concentrate.) Add cardoons and simmer for 15 minutes. Remove to a serving dish and keep warm.

✓ Slice marrow into 1/2-inch rounds. Poach in simmering salted water for 2 minutes. Drain.

✓ Place poached marrow slices over cardoons. Add freshly ground pepper. Serve with the roast .

Chicken in Creamy Cheese Sauce

Poulet à la cancoillotte

The Haute-Saône department, a mostly wooded region, is located in northeastern France, between the Vosges Mountains to the north and the Jura mountains to the south. It forms part of the ancient province of Franche-Comté (free county) spun off from the duchy of Burgundy in the sixth century. Contested and conquered at various times by Burgundy, the Holy Roman Empire, and even Spain, the Franche-Comté along with Burgundy was integrated into France in the seventeenth century.

Cancoillotte, principally produced in the Franche-Comté, Lorraine, and Luxemburg, is a runny cow cheese, low in fat, sold in tubs.

"Simple but irresistibly delicious, this chicken dish is particularly good served with potato galettes."

Patrice Debray
Deputy of Haute-Saône

✓ Preheat oven to 350°F.

✓ Cut chicken into serving pieces. Season, and dredge in flour.

✓ In an ovenproof casserole, heat oil and butter. Brown chicken pieces on all sides. When nicely colored, cover and place chicken in oven to finish cooking, about 30 minutes.

✓ When done, remove casserole from oven and reserve chicken. In same fat, sauté shallots, garlic, and mushrooms. Pour in cognac. Ignite. When flames have subsided, add chicken stock and cook down until reduced by half. Add cream and cancoillotte, stirring while sauce thickens. Taste and adjust seasoning.

✓ Return chicken pieces to sauce. Simmer 5 minutes. Serve at once.

Serves 6–8

1 chicken, 4–5 pounds, cut into 8 pieces
Pepper and salt
2 tablespoons flour
2 tablespoons olive oil
2 tablespoons butter
2 shallots, thinly sliced
2 garlic cloves, minced
1/2 pound white mushrooms, sliced
1 tablespoon cognac
1 cup chicken stock
1 cup heavy cream
1/2 pound cancoillotte

Fougerolles Cherry Cake

Gâteau aux cerises de Fougerolles

"In the Haute-Saône we are lucky to have Fougerolles, the capital of cherries and of their distilled by-product, the famous kirsch.
"This recipe was given to me by my mother, who to this day carries on her cherry dessert tradition with her grandchildren and great-grandchildren. You may replace the cherries with raspberries or black currants."

Michel Raison
Deputy of Haute-Saône

Serves 6

1/2 cup sugar
2/3 cup almond flour
6 tablespoons butter, melted
2 eggs
1 teaspoon vanilla extract
1/2 pound cherries, pitted
Confectioners' sugar (optional)

✓ Preheat oven to 350°F.
✓ In a bowl, mix sugar, almond flour, butter, eggs, and vanilla. Stir in cherries. Pour batter into a buttered baking dish.
✓ Bake 40 minutes.
✓ Sprinkle with confectioners' sugar. Serve.

Chicken in Cream Sauce "Mère Blanc"

Poulet de Bresse à la crème, façon "mère Blanc"

The Bresse chicken is considered the very best there is. This prince of poulets, with white feathers and blue feet, has been raised free in grass fields and fed with corn, milk, and wheat since Roman times. The Bresse region that is its home extends from the river Saône to the Jura Mountains. "The finest chicken in the world, an AOC since 1959, a land of farmers who love their products, an extraordinary and unforgettable dish. Here is the celebrated recipe of Michelin three-star chef Georges Blanc of Bourg-en-Bresse and Vonnas."

Arnaud Montebourg
Deputy of Saône-et-Loire

Serves 4

1 Bresse chicken, or other free-range chicken, about 4 pounds
Pepper and salt
8 tablespoons butter
1 onion, quartered
10 white mushrooms, quartered
2 garlic cloves, unpeeled, smashed
1 bouquet garni
1 cup dry white wine
4 cups heavy cream
1 lemon

✓ Joint the chicken. Cut off wing tips and discard. Cut wings in two. Separate drumsticks from thighs. Cut through breastbone to obtain two filets. Season the chicken pieces.

✓ In a large skillet, melt butter and sauté chicken pieces over high heat. Add onion, mushrooms, garlic, and bouquet garni. When the chicken is well browned on all sides, about 15 minutes altogether, add white wine to deglaze. Let wine reduce, then add cream. Cook over low heat 25–30 minutes. Remove chicken and keep warm.

✓ Strain sauce through a sieve. Add a squeeze of lemon juice. Adjust seasoning.

✓ Put chicken pieces on serving plates, and coat with wine/cream sauce. Serve with steamed rice.

White Sausage with Apples

Boudin blanc aux pommes

The delicate sausage called boudin blanc *(literally, white pudding) is made of cream and the white meat of chicken, or veal with perhaps some pork. Greatly appreciated at all times, it is an indispensable part of Christmas dinner. It can be found in specialty shops and online. This recipe was provided by Fabienne Labrette-Ménager, deputy of Sarthe.*

Serves 4

4 boudin blanc sausages, about
1 pound
4 Gala apples
2 Bartlett pears
3 tablespoons butter
1/4 cup cider vinegar

✓ Cut the sausages in 3/4-inch slices. Peel and core the apples and pears, and quarter them lengthwise.

✓ In a skillet, melt butter. Cook sausage slices with the apple and pear wedges until all become amber color. Remove and place on serving plates.

✓ Deglaze skillet with cider vinegar, and drizzle over each plate. Serve.

Accompany with a well-chilled hard apple cider.

Apple Cake
Gâteau aux pommes

The Sarthe department, named for the largest of its many rivers, is in the Loire country. About half the population lives in the capital, Le Mans, known for its Roman ruins and its automobile races. But the rest of the department, with fairly flat terrain, remains broadly agricultural. This recipe was provided by Béatrice Pavy, deputy of Sarthe.

✓ Preheat oven to 325°F.

✓ First make the batter. In a bowl, whisk eggs with sugar until they turn pale and foamy. Add flour and mix until smooth. Stir in melted butter, then yeast, vanilla, and salt.

✓ Peel and core apples, and cut into thick slices.

✓ Make a caramel directly in the cake pan, melting sugar in 2 tablespoons water. Watch carefully, and remove from heat just as caramel reaches desired color.

✓ Lay apple slices on warm caramel in a spiral or other pleasing pattern. Pour batter over apples.

✓ Bake 45 minutes.

✓ Remove from oven and invert a cake platter over cake pan. Flip over to unmold. Your cake will have a caramelized apple topping.

Serves 6
5 Granny Smith apples
1/2 cup sugar
2 tablespoons water

For the batter:
2 eggs
6 tablespoons sugar
5 tablespoons flour
7 tablespoons butter, melted
2 tablespoons yeast
1/2 teaspoon vanilla extract
Pinch of salt

Savoyard Bread Pudding

Farçon de Séez, ou Farcement

The ancient county of Savoy, encompassing the northern part of the French Alps, grew into a powerful duchy in the fifteenth century with extensive domains. Ironically, in 1861 the original Savoyard lands—now the departments of Savoie and Haute-Savoie—were joined to France, while the House of Savoy assumed the throne of Italy. Now the two Savoy departments welcome a steady flow of tourists drawn by the magnificence of the scenery, the extensiveness of the hiking and ski trails, and the excellence of the Savoyard table.
"This local recipe is a recent prizewinning variation on the very old-fashioned theme of bread pudding."

Hervé Gaymard
Deputy of Savoie

Serves 8

1 pound day-old bread
1/2 cup raisins
1/2 cup dark rum
4 cups milk
3/4 cup sugar
3 cloves
1/2 teaspoon cinnamon
Pinch of saffron
2 eggs, lightly beaten
4 tablespoons butter

✓ Break bread into small pieces in a large bowl.
✓ In a saucepan, heat raisins and rum with 1 cup water. Turn heat off. Reserve.
✓ In another saucepan, heat milk, sugar, cloves, cinnamon, and saffron. When it boils, turn heat off and infuse for 15 minutes.
✓ Pour milk mixture and raisin mixture over bread pieces. Soak for 1 hour.
✓ Add beaten eggs and mix well.
✓ In a skillet, heat butter. Pour contents of bowl into the skillet, tamping down with a fork. Lower heat, and cook until bottom is golden brown and top is solid. Unmold onto a platter.

Serve warm.

Sausages and Onions in White Wine

Diots au vin blanc

Diots (pronounced "djo") are pork sausages native to Savoy. Some are smoked and some are not, some are spicy, others have spinach added to the meat. They are served either grilled, boiled, or prepared in a wine sauce. When served cold, Dijon mustard is the condiment of choice.
"I have selected this traditional recipe for its simplicity of preparation and its savory taste. These diots are especially welcome after a day hiking in the mountains of High Savoy. The onions slowly reduce to a compote, and the sausages go perfectly with potatoes or with crozets, a uniquely Savoyard pasta made of plain or buckwheat flour."

Bernard Accoyer
Deputy of Haute-Savoie

✓ Slice onions thinly.
✓ In a skillet, heat oil and butter. Sauté onions until translucent.
✓ Add flour and cook for 1–2 minutes, then stir wine in, slowly at first while the sauce thickens.
✓ Prick the diots with a fork and add them to the pan. Reduce heat and simmer 20–30 minutes, depending on their size. Serve.

Serves 4

2 large onions
2 tablespoons peanut oil
1 tablespoon butter
1 tablespoon flour
1 bottle white wine from Savoie
4–8 diots, depending on size

Tartare of Smoked and Fresh Lake Fish

Tartare de féra fumée et fraîche du lac Léman

"This Alpine department, famous for its mountains, also possesses two large and important lakes, Annecy and Geneva. Fishing in these richly populated lakes, both for commerce and for sport, is a long-standing tradition. Féra, a whitefish of the salmon family native to Lake Geneva, is a very fine fish, often smoked, and appreciated by lovers of freshwater fish."

Marc Francina
Deputy of Haute-Savoie

Serves 2–4

1 1/3 pounds fresh féra
1/3 pound smoked féra
3 shallots, finely chopped
1/2 cup chives, finely chopped
1/2 pound fingerling potatoes, cooked
4 tablespoons butter
1/2 cup walnuts, chopped
1 cup crème fraiche
2 tablespoons prepared horseradish
Salt
Mesclun or arugula, for garnish

For the vinaigrette:
2/3 cup walnut oil
1/4 cup grapeseed oil
2 tablespoons walnut vinegar
2 tablespoons balsamic vinegar
4 teaspoons walnut mustard (see note)

✓ Finely chop fresh and smoked féra.

✓ In a bowl, whisk all vinaigrette ingredients.

✓ In another bowl, mix fresh and smoked féra with 1 shallot and half the chives. Drizzle 2 tablespoons vinaigrette over fish. Refrigerate.

✓ Cut potatoes into cubes. Sauté in butter until golden. Mix in a bowl with chopped walnuts and remaining vinaigrette, chives, and shallots.

✓ In a chilled bowl, whip heavy cream. Fold in horseradish and a bit of salt.

✓ With a cookie cutter, shape a disc of the fish mixture on each serving plate. Drop a dollop of horseradish cream on top of tartare. Flank with potatoes and a handful of mesclun. Serve.

Note: Walnut mustard is increasingly available in specialty shops. To approximate, stir a spoonful of finely ground toasted walnuts into good-quality Dijon mustard.

Iced Gazpacho
Gaspacho glacé

This recipe was provided by Martine Aurillac, deputy of Paris.

Serves 6

2 slices day-old bread
2 pounds tomatoes, peeled and seeded
1 cucumber, peeled and cubed
1 onion, chopped
3 garlic cloves, minced
2 tablespoons olive oil
1 tablespoon sherry vinegar
1/2 cup basil leaves
1/2 cup cilantro, finely chopped
Pepper and salt
Garlic croutons, for garnish

✓ Prepare garlic croutons and, when cool, wrap and set aside.

✓ Reserve half the cubed cucumber, 1 tablespoon basil, and 1 tablespoon cilantro. Refrigerate.

✓ In the blender, purée all the other ingredients. Taste and adjust seasoning. Refrigerate several hours or overnight.

✓ Serve well chilled, sprinkling with cubed cucumber, a little basil and cilantro, and the croutons.

Broiled Pig's Inner Parts

Tentation de saint Antoine

The Temptation of Saint Anthony is a caloriferous feast of pig's feet, snout, ear, and tail, broiled. Not everyone's taste. But for those who do enjoy "the whole hog," it is a marvel.

"I was introduced to the Temptation of Saint Anthony by my friend Daniel Karrenbauer, owner of the venerable Paris restaurant Chez Paul, in the heart of the Bastille district—and just steps from the rue du Faubourg Saint-Antoine. A gourmet and charcuterie lover, I particularly savor authentic old recipes, and this dish perfectly symbolizes a traditional dish both simple and representative of our gastronomic patrimony."

Patrick Bloche
Deputy of Paris

✓ In France, pig's parts often come already cooked from a charcuterie. However, in America, cook the pig's parts for 2–3 hours in a kettle of boiling salted water with onion, leek, carrot, celery, garlic, bouquet garni, peppercorns, and a good dash of vinegar. Check for doneness occasionally; for instance, the ear may cook faster. As the parts are done, remove and let cool.

✓ Preheat oven to 425°F (unless you prefer to use the broiler).

✓ For breading, line up three flat dishes. Mix flour with pepper and salt in the first. Beat the egg in the second. Place the breadcrumbs in the third. Dip each of the pig parts in flour, first. Egg, second, and lastly, in breadcrumbs. Place the breaded parts on a baking pan.

✓ Bake for about 20 minutes, turning pieces halfway through. If using the broiler, 3 minutes on a side should turn the pieces golden and crisp.

✓ To prepare the Béarnaise sauce: place tarragon, shallot, vinegar, and wine, and reduce by half. Cool.
In the blender, emulsify reduction with egg yolks. Turn to high speed, and add butter, pepper and salt. Reserve, refrigerated.

✓ Serve hot with Béarnaise sauce.

Serves 1

1/2 pig's foot, preferably cooked
1/2 pork snout, preferably cooked
1/2 pig's ear, preferably cooked
1 pig's tail, preferably cooked
1/2 cup flour
Pepper and salt
1 egg
1–2 cups breadcrumbs

Béarnaise sauce

1/4 cup tarragon, finely chopped
1 shallot, finely chopped
1/2 cup champagne vinegar
1/2 cup white wine
3 egg yolks
1 stick butter
Pepper and salt

Chocolate Cake

Gâteau au chocolat

"This recipe comes from my grandmother, who passed it on to my mother. This delicious dessert is a tender memory of my childhood, as well as that of my brothers. And now, my children enjoy it as well."

Bernard Debré
Deputy of Paris

✓ Preheat oven to 350°F.

✓ In a saucepan, melt chocolate and butter (or microwave, carefully, in a bowl). Cool a few minutes. Stir in sugar, flour, and the 3 egg yolks.

✓ In a dry bowl, whip egg whites to stiff consistency. Fold into the chocolate mixture.

✓ Butter and flour a cake pan. Pour in the batter.

✓ Bake 20 minutes. Remove from oven, and cool.

✓ Unmold, dust with confectioners' sugar, and serve.

Serves 6

1/2 pound dark chocolate
1/2 pound butter
1/2 pound sugar
3 eggs, separated
3 tablespoons flour
Confectioners' sugar, for dusting

Baked Endives and Ham
Endives au jambon

"My district covers most of the Bray country, land of cattle raising and dairy products. The cheese called Petit Suisse from Gervais was conceived there. The Neufchâtel cheese, made from Normandy cow's milk, is also produced within the Appellation d'Origine Contrôlée zone which extends all around the city of Neufchâtel-en-Bray. Our territory borders Picardy, and there are plenty of exchanges and points in common between our departments. So I have decided to offer a dish that marries endives, widely cultivated in Picardy, with the cheese symbolic of our Pays de Bray."

Michel Lejeune
Deputy of Seine-Maritime

Serves 6

6 good endives, trimmed, cut in half lengthwise
Juice of 1 lemon
3 tablespoons butter
2 tablespoons flour
2 cups milk
6 tablespoons Neufchâtel cheese, crust removed
1/4 teaspoon grated nutmeg
Pepper and salt
6 large slices of ham, cut in half

✓ In a kettle with boiling salted water and lemon juice, cook endives until just done, about 15 minutes. Refresh in cold water. Drain.

✓ In a saucepan, melt 2 tablespoons butter. Add flour, allow to cook for a few minutes without browning, then whisk in cold milk. Bring to a boil, still whisking. Lower heat and cook for 10 minutes.

✓ Remove from stove. Stir in Neufchâtel cheese, nutmeg, and pepper and salt to taste.

✓ Preheat oven to 350°F.

✓ Roll endives in ham slices and place in a buttered gratin dish. Cover with cream sauce.

✓ Gratinée in oven 20 minutes. Serve.

Filet Mignon with Brie
Filet mignon nappé de brie de Meaux

If Brie connotes the famous cheese, it is not only a cheese. It is a region that includes the cities of Meaux and Melun, and encompasses most of the north-central department of Seine-et-Marne. Near to Paris, the region is agriculturally rich and diverse. It is also known for its architecture (Vaux-le-Vicomte, Fontainebleau) and art (Barbizon).
"I should like to present a dish typical of my region: beef with brie. A testimony to the culinary diversity of France."

Jean-François Copé
Deputy of Seine-Maritime

✓ In a skillet, heat oil and butter. Over high heat, sear the filets quickly on all sides. Turn heat low, cover, and cook gently for 45 minutes.

✓ Meanwhile, with a knife, scrape Brie cheese crust off. Cut cheese into cubes. In a nonstick pan, melt cubes over low heat.

✓ In a glass, mix the cornstarch with 2 teaspoons milk. When the cheese is melted, turn up the heat and stir in the diluted cornstarch, stirring until creamy and smooth. Little by little, add remaining cold milk, stirring constantly. The cheese sauce should become smooth but not heavy, just thick enough to coat a spoon.

✓ When the meat is cooked, cut it in 1/2-inch slices. Place them on a serving platter.

✓ Add the cheese sauce to the meat juices in the pan and heat briefly, stirring to combine well. Pour sauce over meat slices.

✓ Serve hot, with rice or tagliatelle.

<u>Serves 6</u>
1 tablespoon butter
2 tablespoons sunflower oil
2 filets mignons, about 12 ounces each
1/2 pound ripe Brie de Meaux
1 tablespoon cornstarch
1 cup milk
Pepper and salt

Poached Hen "Belle Gabrielle"

Poularde "Belle Gabrielle"

"This recipe is a variation on the poule au pot of Henry IV. This monarch was so attached to our town, Mantes-la-Jolie, that he installed his mistress, the beautiful Gabrielle d'Estrées, there. His chef created this dish for her."

Cécile Dumoulin
Deputy of Yvelines

Serves 6

1 free-range hen, 5–6 pounds
8 carrots
6 turnips
1 kohlrabi
4 leeks
1 bouquet garni
1 onion, studded with 6 cloves
2 garlic cloves, germ removed, minced
Pepper and salt
4 cups crème fraiche

For the "plaisir du galant" stuffing:

1/2 cup parsley, finely chopped
2 garlic cloves, germ removed, minced
2 shallots, finely chopped
1 chicken liver, cut finely
1 chicken gizzard, cut finely
1 slice ham, diced
1 thick slice fatback, cut finely
3 slices day-old bread, soaked in milk, squeezed dry
1 tarragon sprig
3/4 pound pork sausage meat
2 eggs
2 tablespoons crème fraiche
1 cup white fruit alcohol of choice

✓ Prepare the stuffing: In a bowl, combine parsley, shallot, liver, ham, fatback, bread, tarragon, sausage meat, eggs, crème fraiche, and vodka. Refrigerate several hours or overnight.

✓ Remove fowl and marinated stuffing from refrigerator. Stuff the fowl. Wedge a crust of bread into the vent, and sew it up or close with pins.

✓ Peel the carrots, turnips, kohlrabi, and leeks, and cut into moderate pieces.

✓ In a deep kettle, bring water to a boil with the bouquet garni and the onion studded with cloves. When the first bubbles appear, plunge the stuffed fowl in. The water should cover it comfortably. Set the cover halfway on the kettle and let the hen boil for 15 minutes.

✓ Add carrots, leeks, kohlrabi, garlic, pepper and salt. (Do not add turnips. Cook these separately in bouillon taken from pot.) Continue to simmer for 45 minutes, turning the hen over frequently. You may need to add chicken stock during the cooking.

✓ Remove fowl. Cut into serving pieces. Return to kettle for 10 more minutes, together with the crème fraiche, which will cook down.

Serve hot, with wild mushrooms and a vegetable purée.

Macaroons from Niort

Macarons de Niort

There are two rivers called the Sèvres. One is the Sèvres Nantaise, which joins the Loire at Nantes; the other is the Sèvres Niortaise, which passes through Niort on its way to the Atlantic. Both have their source in the department of Deux-Sèvres, in western France in the old province of Poitou. They have no connection with the town of Sèvres on the outskirts of Paris, known for its fine porcelain.

"This delicious macaroon recipe differs from others in that it uses angelica, an aromatic plant that is the gastronomic emblem of the town of Niort. Cultivated and processed in artisanal fashion in Niort and the surrounding Poitou wetlands, angelica is used in making candy, preserves, pastries, and liqueur. I find it especially good in these macaroons. Baking these delicate pastries requires a careful eye on the oven temperature—and instinct born of experience."

Geneviève Gaillard
Deputy of Deux-Sèvres

✓ Preheat oven to 375°F.

✓ With a mortar and pestle, or in a blender, grind almonds with sugar and egg whites.

✓ In a frying pan over low heat, dry the mixture for 10 minutes. Stir. Incorporate angelica.

✓ On a baking sheet lined with parchment paper, drop spoonfuls of the mixture, about the size of a walnut, at least 1 inch apart. Bake 10 minutes. Remove and cool.

Serves 4

1 cup almonds

2 cups sugar

3 egg whites

2 tablespoons candied angelica, cut very fine

Somme Bay Scallop Chowder

Coquillade de la baie de Somme

"Fishermen in the bay of the Somme, out of Hourdel, Crotoy, or Saint-Valery-sur-Somme, all share the habit of keeping a big pot of potatoes, carrots, and onions simmering on their boat's cookstove to feed and warm them. As they pull in their nets with scallops, any unsaleable scallops with broken shells are thrown into the pot, immediately raising the quality of their meals. I have adapted and 'enriched' the original recipe by adding wine, cream, and an egg yolk."

Jérôme Bignon
Deputy of Somme

Serves 4

3 tablespoons olive oil
6 onions, coarsely cut
6 cups fish or vegetable stock
6 potatoes, quartered
4 carrots, cut into chunks
Pepper and salt
16 scallops
2 tablespoons crème fraiche
1 egg yolk
2 cups white wine

✓ In a large kettle, heat olive oil and sauté onions until golden.
✓ Pour in the stock. Add potatoes, carrots, pepper, and salt, and simmer until tender.
✓ In a bowl, mix cream and yolk. Set aside.
✓ When vegetables are cooked, add wine and scallops. Continue to cook over very low heat for 2 1/2 minutes.
✓ Remove from fire. Add cream and yolk. Stir gently.
✓ Adjust seasoning, and serve.

Leek Tart
Flamiche aux poireaux

"A regional specialty of Picardy, flamiche is proudly served in Marie-Christine Klopp's restaurant in Roye. Madame Klopp has been cooking and running the place, following in her mother's tradition, and has maintained her Michelin star for forty years. Her flamiche is the best around, and I am delighted that she agreed to share her recipe."

Alain Gest
Deputy of Somme

Serves 6
4 leeks, well washed
7 tablespoons butter
Pepper and salt
2/3 cup heavy cream
2 egg yolks
2 sheets puff pastry, preferably made with butter

✓ Cut the root ends off the leeks. Slice and then mince the white parts and the lower one-third of the green parts.

✓ In a heavy-bottomed saucepan, slowly melt 4 tablespoons butter, and as soon as it begins to sizzle, add leeks. Season to taste, and cook down, adding a little water from time to time, until the leeks are reduced to a compote. Add remaining 3 tablespoons butter in small bits. When these are well incorporated, add cream and stir to blend. Set aside.

✓ Preheat oven to 350°F.

✓ Roll out puff pastry. Cut six 5-inch circles for the bottoms of the flamiches, and six 6-inch circles for the tops.

✓ On a sturdy baking sheet, slightly moistened, place the six smaller pastry rounds. Divide the leek fondue among them, heaping it in the center. Lightly wet the border of each bottom round, then place a larger round on top of each. Press the edges firmly to seal.

✓ Beat egg yolks with 1 tablespoon water. With a pastry brush, paint tops and borders with this egg wash. If you like, make a design with the point of a knife.

✓ Bake 10 minutes at 350°F. Reduce temperature to 300°F and continue baking 20–25 minutes. At some point after the first 10 minutes, you will want to slip a sheet of aluminum foil over the flamiches, so the pastry becomes crusty without overbrowning.

✓ Serve hot!

Crepe Rolls with Ham and Mushrooms

Ficelle picarde

"The ficelle picarde is a fairly recent entry in our regional gastronomy. It consists of a thin crepe enveloping a mushroom-stuffed slice of ham, which is then put in a gratin dish, covered with a cream sauce, and gratinéed in the oven.

"A few tips: A bit of lemon juice added to the duxelles not only lightens its color, it helps the mushrooms give up their liquid—and don't forget to salt it; salt absorbs water. Taste to make certain it's strongly seasoned, so it will flavor the rest. Incorporating melted butter into the crepe batter will ensure that the crepes don't stick to the pan. Lastly, wait until duxelles and crepes are cold before assembling. Hot and cold elements don't do well together."

Maxime Gremetz
Deputy of Somme

✓ First, make crepe batter. Mix all ingredients in a bowl. Let rest 30–60 minutes.

✓ Meanwhile, make the duxelles. In a skillet, melt butter. Sauté shallots until translucent. Add mushrooms, pepper, salt, and lemon juice. Stir for 2 minutes on high heat to cook off mushroom liquid, then 2 minutes more on medium. Add 3 tablespoons heavy cream and stir. Allow duxelles to rest 2 hours.

✓ When batter has rested, heat a crepe pan or small frying pan, and make 12 crepes, cooking until they are lightly colored on both sides. Set aside to rest for 2 hours.

✓ Preheat oven to 425°F.

✓ Line up crepes on a work surface. Put half a slice of ham on each. Place a dollop of duxelles on the ham, nudging it into a sausage shape. Roll crepe and ham firmly into a tube. Repeat for each crepe.

✓ Butter a rectangular baking dish. Place crepes, side by side, seam down. (You may opt to use individual gratin dishes. You'll then put 2 crepes in each and cook the same way.) Pour 1/2 cup heavy cream over crepes. Spread Gruyère cheese on top.

✓ Place gratin dish(es) under the broiler for 3 minutes, then move to a middle rack and finish for 5 minutes at 425°F until top is golden and crisp and cream is bubbling.

✓ You may also simply put the dish in the oven, and let it become golden within 20 minutes.

✓ Allow to cool slightly. Serve.

Serves 6

For the crepes:

1 cup milk
1 cup flour
2 eggs
3 tablespoons melted butter
Pepper and salt

For the filling:

2 shallots, minced
2 tablespoons butter
1/2 pound white mushrooms, minced
Pepper and salt
2 drops lemon juice
3 tablespoons heavy cream
6 slices ham
1/2 cup heavy cream
1 cup grated Gruyère cheese

Water-Gardeners' Vegetable Soup

Soupe des hortillons

Hortillons *are market gardeners who grow their wares on parcels of marshy land connected by a grid of canals just outside Amiens, in the Somme department. Vegetables from these lush* hortillonnages *are known to be exceptional in quality and variety.*

"In the year 0, there was a conflict between the Roman gardeners with their hortus *and the Gaulish gardeners with their* jarde. *The horticulturists of the* hortus *won. The gardeners of the* jarde *benefited from their delicious soup."*

Olivier Jarde
Deputy of Somme

Serves 4

1 Savoy cabbage
4 leeks, white only, well washed
3 tablespoons butter
4 cups chicken stock
1/2 pound potatoes, diced small
1 pound petits pois, fresh or, if not available, frozen
1 head Boston lettuce
4 thick slices whole-grain bread, toasted

✓ Core the cabbage, remove rib from each leaf, and shred leaves. Slice the leeks.

✓ In a kettle, heat 2 tablespoons butter and cook cabbage and leeks for 5 minutes. Pour in stock and bring to a boil. Add potatoes and petits pois. Simmer for about 20 minutes. Taste as you go: potatoes should still be firm.

✓ Skim out the vegetables, to preserve their color. Continue to simmer the broth to concentrate its flavor.

✓ Meanwhile, core the lettuce and remove the ribs. In a skillet, melt 1 tablespoon butter. Cook lettuce until it wilts, 30 seconds.

✓ One minute before serving, add lettuce to soup pot, and return other vegetables to reheat.

✓ Put bread at the bottom of soup tureen. Pour soup over. Serve.

Fava Bean Cassoulet

Févoulet avec sa crème d'ail rose de Lautrec

The beautiful, mountainous and forested Tarn department is at the southern edge of the Massif Central. Its capital Albi, on the river Tarn, was a center of the Cathar sect that was put down in the bloody Albigensian Crusade eight centuries ago. Already in those days févoulet *was a staple food.*

"The dish I offer here is a cassoulet made with fèves*, broad or fava beans. In the Middle Ages it was a popular main course in our region. This variant of the now classic white-bean cassoulet is very much part of our local tradition, and good for all occasions."*

Bernard Carayon
Deputy of Tarn

✓ Fava beans do not need presoaking. Immerse them in cold water. Bring to a boil. Drain.

✓ Mince garlic and fatback into a paste.

✓ In a stockpot, put pork rind, pig's foot, hock, onion with cloves, bouquet garni, carrot, leek, celery, garlic-fatback paste, pepper, and salt. Add water to cover by 2 inches. Bring to a boil, and simmer for 1 hour.

✓ Strain stock into a kettle. There should be twice as much stock as beans. Add beans and tomato paste to kettle, along with pig's foot, hock, and strips of rind. Discard remaining solids from strainer.

✓ Cook 1 1/2 hours over very low heat, so beans do not break up.

✓ Meanwhile, make the garlic cream: In a small saucepan, heat 2/3 cup olive oil with pink garlic and poach for 45 minutes. Remove garlic. When cool, discard skins and mash pulp in a bowl. Mix in crème fraiche. In a small pan, heat 1 tablespoon oil and cook onion until cleared. Stir in garlic-cream mixture and heat gently. Pour into serving bowl to be passed with *févoulet*.

✓ In a skillet, place goose confit, coated in the fat it was preserved in. Heat until fat has melted and goose pieces are hot through. Remove goose to a large serving dish. Keep warm.

✓ In same skillet, cook spareribs in goose fat. Remove ribs to serving dish with goose pieces and keep warm.

✓ Lastly, still in goose fat, cook sausage. Remove, cut into 2-inch segments, and add to serving dish.

✓ Take pig's foot, hock, and rind from kettle, discard bones, and stir cut-up meat back into beans.

✓ Ladle beans over meats in serving dish to complete the *févoulet*.

✓ Serve with garlic cream.

Serves 8–10

8 cups fava beans, fresh (shelled) or frozen
2 garlic cloves
1-2 ounces pork fatback
1/2 pound pork rind, cut in broad strips
1 pig's foot
4 duck thighs
1/2 pound pork rind, boiled 15 minutes and drained
1/2 pound fresh pork hock
1 onion, studded with 3 cloves
1 bouquet garni (thyme sprigs, bay leaves)
1 carrot
1 leek
1 stalk celery
Pepper and salt
2 tablespoons tomato paste
1 1/2 pounds confit of goose or, if unavailable, duck
1 pound pork spareribs, separated
1 1/2 pounds fresh Toulouse sausage, or mild Italian sausage

For the garlic cream:
2/3 cup olive oil
1/2 head pink garlic, preferably from Lautrec
1/3 cup heavy cream
1 small onion, minced

"Maw-Breaker" Buns
"Casse-Museaux" de Brassac

"In the southern part of the Massif Central, nestled in the valley of the river Agout between the Causse Noir and the Cévennes, at the heart of the granitic massif of Sidobre, lies the Pays de Brassac."

[According to ancient legend, La Tarasque, a bloodthirsty beast like a dragon, inhabited the river and feasted on passers-by. Her bad moods would trigger terrible floods, chasing the villagers up the mountain. To conquer the beast, it was decided to exploit her weakness: eating. After much discussion, the pâtissier was elected. Each day he lowered from the bridge a basket of aromatic pastry, both tender and crunchy. La Tarasque gobbled enthusiastically and plunged back into the river, replete. But that solution didn't satisfy the village, for while the pâtissier was dealing successfully with the dragon problem, he neglected his other pastries. He set out to invent yet another cake, this one with a crust of stone. When he lowered it into the river, La Tarasque eagerly reached for it, but the crust of stone broke her snout and all 320 of her teeth. She has never been seen since. The pâtissier subsequently modified his recipe, which has become Brassac's great specialty under its name of origin: the Casse-Museau (muzzle-breaker).—Tr.]

"This cake whose recipe dates back to the Middle Ages is reminiscent of its Greek ancestor, l'Orizille, that consisted of mashed wheat mixed with a kind of farmer cheese, honey, lard, and spices. Brassac bakers modernized the recipe, making it a favorite of elderly citizens as they shared it each week while playing games and enjoying wine.

"Mr. Carayon, baker at Brassac, has kindly parted with his modern version of the Casse-Museau."

Philippe Folliot
Deputy of Tarn

Serves 16

6 quarts ewe's milk, or goat milk
1 teaspoon liquid rennet, or 1 tablet
1 1/4 cups flour
2 tablespoons dry yeast
Zest of 1 lemon, grated
8 eggs
Confectioners' sugar for dusting

✓ First, make cheese curd. Have milk tepid, around 90°F. (Do not heat large pot directly on stove, which risks scalding. In a double boiler or microwave, heat a bit at a time—do not boil!—and stir back into rest of milk until warm enough.)

✓ Stir rennet into milk. Leave undisturbed until curds and whey separate, perhaps an hour or more.

✓ Line a large sieve with doubled cheesecloth or muslin, and drain curd.

✓ Preheat oven to 450°F.

✓ In a large bowl, mix flour, yeast, lemon zest, eggs, and cheese curd. Knead well.

✓ Divide dough into 12-ounce portions and form into balls. Place on a baking sheet lined with buttered parchment paper. Bake 10 minutes.

✓ Remove from oven and reduce temperature to 275°F. With scissors, snip a cross on top of each bun. Return to oven and bake another 20 minutes.

✓ Cool a little. Sprinkle with confectioners' sugar. Serve.

Foie Gras with Chasselas Grapes

Foie gras poêlé aux raisins de Chasselas

The Tarn-et-Garonne department is in the southwest of France, the land of foie gras. And the area around Moissac, where the Tarn and Garonne Rivers meet, is the center of cultivation of the AOC-labeled white table grape known as chasselas de Moissac.
"A fertile and generous land, bathed in sunshine, Tarn-et-Garonne brings in one recipe two exceptional products born of our passion."

Sylvia Pinel
Deputy of Tarn-et-Garonne

✓ Wash the grapes. Press one-quarter of them into juice.
✓ Place 4 serving plates in a warming oven.
✓ Cut foie gras into 4 thick slices. Heat a nonstick skillet without any fat (turn fan on). Cook foie gras slices about 2 minutes on each side. Remove slices, cover with foil, and keep warm.
✓ Pour off rendered fat (reserve for another use) and wipe pan. Heat sugar and grapes until lightly caramelized. Deglaze with fresh grape juice. Season to taste.
✓ Place a slice of foie gras on each warmed plate, surrounded with grapes and sauce. Sprinkle with coarsely ground pepper. Serve.

Serves 4

1 pound white table grapes, preferably chasselas
1 pound fresh duck foie gras, in a single lobe
3 tablespoons sugar
Pepper and salt
1 tablespoon coarsely ground pepper

Tomato Tart
Tarte à la tomate

The Var department, in the southeastern Provence-Alpes-Côte d'Azur region, boasts a prime stretch of Mediterranean coast, from the great naval base at Toulon eastward through a host of resort towns—Hyères, Le Lavandou, Saint-Tropez, Sainte-Maxime, Saint-Raphaël . . .
"I especially enjoy preparing this tart in summertime. It is light and succulent and can be served either as a main course, accompanied by a green salad, or as a lovely starter. Its crust is made with pâte brisée."

Josette Pons
Deputy of Var

Serves 6
For the pâte brisée:
1 1/4 cups flour
7 tablespoons butter
4 tablespoons ice water
1/2 teaspoon salt
For the filling:
2 tablespoons Dijon mustard
1/2 pound Gruyère or Comté cheese
5 Roma tomatoes
Pepper and salt
1/2 teaspoon oregano
1 tablespoon olive oil

✔ In a bowl or food processor, combine ingredients and make a ball of dough. Cover in plastic wrap and refrigerate for 30 minutes.
✔ Preheat oven to 400°F.
✔ Roll out dough and line a tart mold. Prick with a fork. Spread mustard over pie crust.
✔ Shave cheese into thin slices with a cheese slicer or a mandoline. Distribute cheese over mustard in tart mold. Slice tomatoes and place on top of cheese layer. Sprinkle with pepper, salt, and oregano. Lastly, trickle olive oil over the top. Place in oven for about 30 minutes. Start checking after 20 minutes. If the tart edges are nicely browned, the tart is cooked. If it appears too pale, continue baking an additional 5–10 minutes. Serve warm.

Fish Soup with Aioli
Bourride toulonnaise

Bourride is one of those dishes that have as many variants as there are cooks. You need a pound per person (cleaned weight, heads and tails off) of fleshy white Mediterranean fish—sea bass, monkfish, John Dory, daurade, turbot, grouper, whiting, hake. The bread may be plain or toasted or fried. The fish may arrive with the soup or soon after. There may be potatoes. The aioli may be supplemented by rouille (see cuttlefish recipe, page 108) and/or shredded cheese. The one constant is the aioli-yolk enrichment that elevates the soup to sumptuous.
"Original, refined, easy to digest, it is sometimes called the bouillabaisse of the poor."

Philippe Vitel
Deputy of Var

✓ Make the aioli in a large mortar. Mash garlic cloves to a paste. Stirring constantly with the pestle always in the same direction, add salt and 1 egg yolk, then slowly begin to trickle oil in. As the mixture thickens, after 3–4 tablespoons of oil, stir in lemon juice and 1/2 teaspoon warm water, then resume stirring oil in, bit by bit. Each time sauce feels too thick, again add a few drops of warm water; this will prevent separation. (However, if the aioli does "break," it can be rescued. Scrape it into a bowl and clean the mortar. Place in the mortar an extra yolk and a bit more lemon juice and then, stirring constantly with the pestle, reincorporate the broken aioli slowly, spoon by spoon.)

✓ Reserve half the aioli in a mixing bowl, and place half in a sauceboat for the table.

✓ Cut the fish into chunks of about 3 inches.

✓ Place a serving dish in a warming oven.

✓ Tie together the bay leaf, thyme, fennel, and orange peel to make a bouquet garni.

✓ In a large kettle, place fish, onion, bouquet garni, pepper, and salt. Add hot water (or stock, if you had fishheads) to cover well. Bring to a boil and reduce to simmer. After 10 minutes, as various fish are done, remove to serving dish and keep warm. Discard bouquet garni. If desired, boil down stock somewhat. Remove from heat.

✓ In bowl with reserved aioli, stir in 1 cup fish stock and 4 egg yolks. Whisk aioli-yolk mixture into soup, stirring over low heat until it starts to thicken. Do not boil.

✓ In each soup plate, place 1–2 pieces of toast and a ladle of soup. Pour rest of soup into a tureen and send to table with fish, remaining toast, aioli—and a hearty "Help yourselves!"

A white wine from Bandol or Pierrefeu is recommended.

Serves 4
For the aioli:
8 garlic cloves
Pinch of salt
1–2 egg yolks
1 cup olive oil
Juice of 1 lemon
Warm water

For the soup:
4–5 pounds assorted white fish
1 bay leaf
2–3 sprigs thyme
2–3 stalks wild fennel, or fronds from bulb fennel
Zest of 1 orange
2 onions, chopped
Pepper and salt
4–8 cups hot water
4 egg yolks
8–12 slices French bread, toasted

Melon Tiramisu

Tiramisu au melon de Cavaillon

Cavaillon, a Provençal market town on the river Durance, the southern border of the Vaucluse department, was long ago anointed Capital of Melons. For many decades, most melons in France and Europe came from Cavaillon. All sorts of lore accompany the Cavaillon melon. Some claim the popes brought it to France from Italy in the fourteenth century when they resided in Avignon. Some insist that to choose a good Cavaillon melon, you must count the stripes—there should be exactly ten, no more, no less—and the stripes must be bluish-green. There is now a Confrérie des Chevaliers de l'Ordre du Melon de Cavaillon/Brotherhood of the Knights of the Order of the Cavaillon Melon. And in summertime there is the inevitable Fête des Melons. This recipe was provided by Jean-Claude Bouchet, deputy of Vaucluse.

Serves 12

1 melon, Cavaillon or cantaloupe
1 1/2 cups sugar
3 tablespoons melon liqueur
24 ladyfingers
6 eggs, separated
1 pound mascarpone

✓ Remove seeds and skin, and cut melon into 1/2-inch cubes.
✓ Make a sugar syrup by boiling 3/4 cup sugar with 1 1/2 cups water. Add 1 tablespoon melon liqueur. Place in a flat-bottomed bowl. Cool until tepid.
✓ Soak ladyfingers in melon syrup. Line bottom of a serving bowl, or individual stemmed dessert glasses, with ladyfingers. Sprinkle with melon cubes.
✓ Whip egg whites until stiff, adding remaining 2 tablespoons liqueur.
✓ In a separate bowl, whisk egg yolks with remaining 3/4 cups sugar and mascarpone until pale and foamy.
✓ Fill serving bowl or individual glasses with alternating layers of whipped whites and yolks. Serve.

Rennet Pudding from the Vendée

Caillebottes

"Well known in the Vendée, caillebottes used to be served at daily meals as well as at weddings and christenings. Milk is coagulated (caillé) into clumps (bottes) of curd by adding rennet (présure). In the old days, people used the flowers of the chardonnette, a sort of wild artichoke that grows on our coastal dunes, as the coagulant. Traditionalists, and vegetarians, may look for the dried flowers at an herbalist. Regular rennet, made from a calf's stomach, comes in liquid or tablet form.

"This dessert was a memorable part of my childhood. Rather like yogurt in texture, it is easy to afford, to prepare, to digest, and, best of all, to vary with the addition of coffee or cinnamon or vanilla or any flavor you wish."

Véronique Besse
Deputy of Vendée

✓ In a saucepan, heat 3 cups milk just to lukewarm. Add salt, rennet, and 2 tablespoons sugar. Mix well, cover, and leave for 1 hour to let the curd set.

✓ Meanwhile, boil the remaining 1 cup milk. Add cinnamon, vanilla, and remaining sugar. Allow to cool completely. Remove cinnamon stick.

✓ When the curd has set—the surface will have solidified—make crisscross cuts with a knife right into the pan. Put the pan back on the fire. The whey will quickly rise to the surface. Pour it off.

✓ Let the *caillebottes* cool completely. Mix in the boiled and flavored milk. Chill.

✓ It will keep in the refrigerator for a day—or more, reportedly, though I have not seen this put to the test.

Serves 4

1 quart unpasteurized milk
4 grains sea salt
4 drops liquid rennet
1 cup sugar
1 stick cinnamon
1 teaspoon vanilla

Ham with White Beans
Jambon aux mogettes

On the Atlantic coast, the Vendée is at the western end of the Loire country. Bracketed by the Marais Breton and the Marais Potevin, former wetlands now largely converted to polder, the rest of the department is bocage, a region of fields and meadows demarcated by hedgerows or lines of trees and punctated by rural hamlets and farmsteads. With its fishing industry and mussels and oysters beds along the coast, the Vendée has everything to tempt the palate.

"*This traditional recipe is an institution for everyone born in the Vendée, a cultural monument. Our white bean called the mogette is the product most emblematic of our* terroir. *As is often the case with good things,* jambon-mogettes *consists of simple ingredients and is easy to prepare.*"

Dominique Souchet
Deputy of Vendée

Serves 4

1 pound white beans
4 tablespoons butter
1 carrot, peeled and sliced
1 onion, chopped
2 garlic cloves, minced
1 bouquet garni
Pepper and salt
4 thick slices cooked ham

✓ Soak white beans in water for 24 hours. Drain.

✓ Bring water to a boil and plunge the beans in. Cook 5 minutes. Drain,

✓ In a heavy saucepan, melt butter and sauté beans over low heat. Add carrot, onion, garlic, and bouquet garni. Cover with cold water. Bring to a boil, reduce heat, and simmer covered for 1 1/2 hours. Midway through the cooking, add pepper and salt to taste.

✓ Sauté ham 2 minutes on each side. Serve with beans.

Sugar Galette
Broyé du Poitou

The departments of Vienne and Haute-Vienne are named after the river Vienne, which winds its way through both (with a detour into the Charente department) on its way north to join the river Loire. The Vienne and its capital, Poitiers, are the heart of the ancient province of Poitou, one of the vast lands that Eleanor of Aquitaine brought by marriage to the English crown. But it has been squarely back in French hands since the fourteenth century. This recipe may be almost that old.

"A specialty of Poitou and especially of the Vienne, the broyé *("smashed") owes its name to an ancestral practice, the dividing-up of this sturdy and supersized cookie with a sharp blow of the fist. Made with the renowned local butter, and lent a distinctive taste by a pinch of salt from the Charente-Maritime salt marshes, the broken* broyé *was traditionally offered at church after Mass, weddings, and Communions. One of my childhood memories is the inviting aroma of the* broyé *coming out of the oven, and the choosing of the pieces we would have for our Sunday afternoon snack."*

Jean-Pierre Abelin
Deputy of Vienne

✓ Preheat oven to 350°F.

✓ In a bowl, mix all ingredients except yolk. Do not knead too much. (If using a food processor, pulse.)

✓ On a sheet of parchment paper, roll out dough into a single large round. Neaten up the edges. Lift parchment and dough directly onto a baking sheet. Make decorative stripes on the dough with a fork or knife. Beat egg yolk with a little water, and apply this wash to dough with a pastry brush.

✓ Bake 25–30 minutes. Remove from oven, allow to cool, and give a sharp whack in the middle. Follow up with further whacks as needed. Serve.

✓ Uneaten pieces should be stored in a closed cookie tin to retain crispness.

Serves 6

3 cups flour
1 1/4 cups sugar
1/2 pound butter, preferably Poitou-Charentes
1/2 teaspoon sea salt
Eau-de-vie of choice (optional)
1 egg plus 1 yolk

Cherry Clafoutis
Clafoutis aux cerises

The Haute-Vienne department in west-central France occupies a large part of the region historically called the Limousin. Their mutual capital, Limoges, has long been famous for its porcelain manufacture—producing fine dinnerware on which to serve fine Limousin cuisine.

"We two agree that the clafoutis is the perfect Limousin signature dessert, easy to prepare and always delicious, served warm or cold. While cherries are the basis of the original recipe, clafoutis can be made with cut-up pears, apricots, apples—or plums, in which case it is called flognarde limousine. *If you wish, you may add to the batter a spoonful of rum or an eau-de-vie, such as kirsch, to go with cherries."*

Daniel Boisserie
Marie-Françoise Pérol-Dumont
Deputies of Haute-Vienne

Serves 4
4 tablespoons butter
1 cup milk
3 eggs
1/2 cup sugar
Pinch of salt
1 teaspoon vanilla extract
1/3 cup flour
1/2 tablespoon dry yeast
1/3 cup crème fraiche
1 pound cherries, washed, stemmed, and pitted

✓ Preheat oven to 350°F.
✓ Butter a gratin dish. Melt the rest of the butter. Warm the milk.
✓ In a bowl, whisk eggs with sugar, salt, and vanilla until pale. Gently stir in flour and yeast. Still stirring, incorporate melted butter and crème fraiche. Stir in warm milk.
✓ Distribute cherries in gratin dish and pour batter over them.
✓ Bake 35 minutes. Serve.

Pâté from Lorraine
Pâté lorrain

The Vosges department, in Lorraine in the northeast of France, is named after the mountain range that separates Lorraine from its eastern neighbor Alsace. Among the tourist attractions are Domrémy, birthplace of Joan of Arc, and the thermal spa towns of Vittel and Contrexéville, whose mineral waters are being exported throughout the world.

"Every Sunday during my childhood, wafts of my mother's culinary wonders filled the house in anticipation of our weekly family gathering. I particularly remember the aroma of her pâté as it came out of the oven with its golden crust, and how hard it was to wait to taste it. Years later I happened upon the same pâté lorrain *in a small Vosges inn, l'Auberge du Val Joli in Le Valtin, where Philippe Laruelle is exploring the bounty of our Vosges' native products even as he is carrying on with talent his father Jacques's (and my mother's) culinary tradition."*

Gérard Cherpion
Deputy of Vosges

Serves 5
1/2 pound veal
1/2 pound pork
2 shallots, finely chopped
1 cup parsley, finely chopped
1 bottle white wine
Pepper and salt
2 sheets puff pastry
1 egg yolk

✓ Preheat oven to 400°F.

✓ Cut veal and pork into thin strips. In a bowl, mix meats, shallots, parsley, wine, pepper, and salt. Cover and refrigerate overnight or longer.

✓ On a floured work surface, roll out two-thirds of the puff pastry into a rectangle. Remove meats from marinade. Place neatly in the middle of the rectangle, leaving a 1-inch border all around. Fold up the sides and ends and pinch the corners, to encase the meat in a basket of pastry.

✓ Roll out remaining puff pastry to form a top crust. Place over meat. Pinch edges of top and bottom pastry together tightly. With a pastry brush, "paint" top and sides with yolk. Cut two holes for "chimneys" to let steam out.

✓ You may cut a little extra puff pastry into leaves or other decorations and apply on top, painting these as well.

✓ Bake 15 minutes. Reduce temperature to 350°F. Continue baking 45 more minutes.

✓ Serve hot, accompanied by a green salad.

Vosges Trout with Herbs

Truite des Vosges aux herbes

"My friend Jean-Claude Aiguier, a great chef who is devoted to using the products of his native Vosges, gave me this recipe. It is a variation on the classic truite au bleu, *in which the freshly killed and gutted trout is poached in a court bouillon containing vinegar, which turns the skin blue."*

François Vannson
Deputy of Vosges

✓ Ideally, you will bring trout home alive. If they are killed and gutted by the fishmonger, cook as soon as possible. Until then, leave in wax paper; do not wipe with paper towel, which will damage the skin.

✓ In a heavy-bottomed oval casserole that will just hold the trout, heat lemon juice, water, butter, pepper, and salt. When butter is melted and water bubbling, place trout in casserole, belly down, head to tail.

✓ Cover and poach over moderately high heat for 7 minutes. Test with a paring knife: if flesh comes away from backbone, fish is done; if not, try again after 1–2 minutes.

✓ Add herbs, replace cover, and cook for 1 minute more.

Serve with steamed or boiled potatoes, and a white auxerrois de Toul. (Despite its name, the auxerrois grape is not from Burgundy but from Lorraine.)

Serves 4

4 trout, freshly killed and gutted
Juice of 2 lemons
1 cup water
1 stick butter
Pepper and salt
1 bunch chives, roughly chopped
1 bunch chervil, roughly chopped
1 bunch flat parsley, roughly chopped
1 bunch dill, roughly chopped
2 tarragon sprigs, leaves stripped from stems and chopped

Cheese Puffs
Gougères

Named after the river Yonne that flows north to meet the Seine, the Yonne department in north-central France forms the upper-left quadrant of Burgundy. Unsurprisingly, there are towns in the Yonne—Auxerre, Avallon, Chablis, Joigny, Vézelay—with cuisine to match the area's wines. "For us both, deputies of Yonne, this Burgundy specialty made of choux pastry with cheese such as Comté or Emmental is a perfect accompaniment to Kir, the aperitif of Chablis wine laced with black currant liqueur. More generously sized, gougères can be served as a first course, with a fine Burgundy wine. The gougère was created by a Parisian pâtissier by the name of Hénard who moved to Flogny-la-Chapelle in the eighteenth century and who modified the Parisian ramequin then in vogue into these freestanding little savory puffs that may be enjoyed either warm or cold."

Marie-Louise Fort
Jean-Marie Rolland
Deputies of Yonne

Serves 4
1 cup water
8 tablespoons butter
Pinch of salt
Pepper
1 cup flour
4 large eggs
1 cup grated Gruyère or Comté

✓ Preheat oven to 400°F.

✓ In a saucepan, bring to a boil water, butter, salt, pepper. When butter is melted and water boils, remove from fire and put flour in all at once, stirring vigorously. Return to fire and stir until dough detaches itself from sides of pot. Set aside to cool until tepid.

✓ Add eggs one at a time while continuing to stir to achieve a smooth paste. Stir in cheese, reserving a small amount for topping.

✓ Line a large baking sheet, or two, with parchment paper. Divide dough into small balls, the size of a ping-pong ball, and place 1 1/2 inches apart. Sprinkle tops with remaining cheese. (Or you can opt to cut thin strips of cheese and place one or two on top.)

✓ Bake 25–30 minutes until gougères are puffed high, and golden. Serve.

Spit-Roasted Pig's Head
Tête de porc à la broche

"In my political career, first as minister of tourism, then as minister of agriculture, gastronomy was one of my occupational concerns. My friend Marc Meneau, the celebrated chef of Vézelay, has kindly shared his recipe for barbecued pig's head, one of my favorite dishes. While it is normally a rather intricate process, over time I have simplified its details. I know this dish is not to everyone's taste. For the adventurous, however, I highly recommend it."

Jean-Pierre Soisson
Deputy of Yonne

Serves 4

1 pig's head
1 pork tongue, front part only
1 lemon, halved
Pepper and salt
1/2 cup Dijon mustard
1/2 cup parsley, chopped
1/2 cup chervil, chopped
1 tablespoon tarragon leaves, chopped
1 cup sifted flour
5 eggs and 5 yolks
1–2 cups fine breadcrumbs
4 tablespoons butter
1 bunch watercress, washed

For the broth:

1/4 cup flour
2 cups white wine
2–3 quarts water
2 carrots
2 medium onions, studded with cloves
4 leeks
2 shallots
5 garlic cloves
1 bouquet garni
Kosher salt
Peppercorns

✓ Soak pig's head and tongue in ice water for 2 hours.

✓ Rub head with lemon. Blanch head and tongue, refresh in cold water, and rinse.

✓ Make the broth. In a bowl, mix white wine with flour. In a large kettle, place water, remaining broth ingredients, and the wine-flour mixture (for a process called *cuire dans un blanc*).

✓ Place head and tongue in broth, bring to a boil, and simmer for 2 1/2 hours. Add water as needed, so meats remain covered.

✓ Remove cooked meats to a carving board, pressing the head to flatten. Cut off ears, and trim head into a neat rectangle. Discard visible layers of fat. Season the head, spread mustard all over, and sprinkle with parsley, chervil, and tarragon.

✓ While still hot, peel skin from tongue. Cut lengthwise. Place tongue halves in center of rectangle.

✓ Lift rectangle onto a large piece of plastic wrap. Roll meats tightly into a sausage shape, compressing as much as possible. Encase firmly in plastic wrap, securing both ends and the middle with twine. Refrigerate at least 6 hours.

✓ Set out three large, flat bowls for breading. Put sifted flour in the first, beaten eggs and yolks in the second, and breadcrumbs in the third.

✓ Remove pig's head from refrigerator and unwrap. Roll in flour. Next, dip into beaten eggs. Lastly, roll in breadcrumbs. Refrigerate for 1 hour. Repeat egg-and-breadcrumb operation twice more, each time with an interval of 1 hour between. After the third breading, the pig's head is ready for use. Keep refrigerated. (All these steps can be done 1 or even 2 days ahead.)

✓ Light the fire for spit roasting. When it is hot, also preheat indoor oven to 350°F. (If you will be spit-roasting on an electric rotisserie within your regular oven, adjust following steps accordingly.)

✓ Place pig's head on spit and set it to turning before the fire. Baste from time to time with melted butter. When it is crisp and golden, after 20–30 minutes, remove from spit. Wrap in aluminum foil, and continue cooking in the 350°F oven for 15 minutes.

✓ Place on serving platter. Slice, and decorate with watercress bunches. Pour cooking juices from the drip pan into a sauceboat to pass separately. Serve.

Blueberry Tart

Tarte aux brimbelles

The territory of Belfort is a department of the Franche-Comté region—a very small one, less than 250 square miles extending from the Swiss border to the southern edge of the Vosges Mountains. It gained its odd designation "territory" in 1871 when it remained part of France while most of Alsace, including the rest of its former department, Haut-Rhin, was taken over by Germany for the next half century.

"Brimbelles—the local term for our delicious wild blueberries—are found throughout the Vosges. As a little boy, I would take long walks with my parents on the mountain called Ballon d'Alsace, and on the way home we always stopped at a small inn for a piece of this tart."

Damien Meslot
Deputy of Belfort Territory

✓ In a bowl, mix all pastry ingredients, forming a smooth dough. Cover with plastic wrap and refrigerate for 1 hour.
✓ Preheat oven to 400°F.
✓ Roll out the dough and line a buttered, floured tart mold. Sprinkle the bottom with cookie crumbs or semolina. Spread blueberries on top. Bake for 20 minutes.
✓ In a bowl beat eggs with sugar and crème fraiche. Remove tart from oven and pour mixture over blueberries. Continue baking another 15–20 minutes. Serve.

Serves 6

For the pastry:
1 1/4 cups flour
6 tablespoons butter
1 tablespoon sugar
1/4 teaspoon salt
1 egg yolk
1/4 cup ice water

For the filling:
2 vanilla cookies, crumbled, or 2 tablespoons fine semolina
1 pound blueberries
2 eggs
1/2 cup sugar
1/4 cup crème fraiche

Cream of Tomato Soup

Velouté de tomates

The Essonne department, named after a tributary of the Seine, is in the Île-de-France region, only a few miles south of Paris. "Known for its cultivation of fruit and vegetables, our land excels particularly in the production of tomatoes—so rich and so good, in fact, that each year in September the town of Montlhéry hosts a Tomato Festival.
"My recipe is very flavorful, economical, and easy to prepare for the enjoyment of everyone around the table."

Françoise Briand
Deputy of Essonne

Serves 4

1 pound ripe tomatoes
4 potatoes
1 carrot
4 garlic cloves, minced
1 onion, minced
2 tablespoons olive oil
5 cups vegetable stock
Pepper and salt
Fresh herbs of choice
Crème fraiche (optional)

✓ Chop the tomatoes. Peel and dice the potatoes and carrot.
✓ In a kettle, heat olive oil. Sauté onion and garlic until translucent. Add tomatoes, potatoes, carrot, and stock. Cover and cook 30 minutes.
✓ Cool a little and purée in the blender. Season to taste. Chop and add one or more fresh herbs (parsley, cilantro, thyme, basil . . .).
✓ Serve. Offer crème fraiche on the side.

Tagliatelle with Truffles and Foie Gras

Tagliatelles à la truffe et aux copeaux de foie gras

The almost entirely urban Hauts-de-Seine department curves around the entire western half of the city of Paris, and is embraced in turn by a long bend of the upper part of the river Seine as it emerges from Paris on its serpentine way to the sea.

"Friendship is as uncomplicated as sharing a bowl of pasta. If that pasta happens to be succulent, it only reinforces the conviviality. This extremely simple recipe comes from my place of origin: the Périgord, where foie gras abounds along with the famous truffle. You won't merely impress your guests with this dish, you will indulge them. Isn't that one of the secrets of perfect hospitality?"

Patrick Ollier
Deputy of Hauts-de-Seine

✓ Gently brush the truffle. Shave into fine slices. In a bowl, combine crème fraiche and truffle. Cover and refrigerate overnight.

✓ The next day, drain truffle slices. Reserve crème fraiche.

✓ Cut two-thirds of foie gras into small cubes. Thinly slice the rest.

✓ In a saucepan, bring stock to a boil and reduce to a simmer. Warm Armagnac in a ladle, ignite, and after flames subside, pour into stock. Stir in truffle-flavored cream, any juice exuded by the truffles, pepper, and salt.

✓ Add cubed foie gras and let melt in simmering sauce for 10 minutes. Adjust seasoning.

✓ Chop some of the chives and parsley, and add with moderation. Keep sauce warm.

✓ Place 4 plates in a warming oven.

✓ In a kettle, bring water and salt to a boil. Cook fresh tagliatelle 2–3 minutes, just until al dente. Drain. Return to kettle, add olive oil, and toss.

✓ On each plate, put a portion of tagliatelle. Coat generously with sauce. Cover with thin slices of truffle, then with slices of foie gras. Sprinkle grains of fleur de sel over the foie gras. Garnish with a few sprigs of parsley and spears of chive. Serve.

Serves 4

1 black truffle, about 1 ounce
1 1/4 cups crème fraiche
2/3 cup veal or beef stock
1/4 cup Armagnac
1/2 pound fresh foie gras
Pepper and salt
1 bunch chives
1/2 cup flat parsley
1 pound fresh tagliatelle
2 tablespoons olive oil
Fleur de sel, or kosher salt

Curried Chicken

Poulet au curry

A mostly urbanized department in the Île-de-France region, Seine-Saint-Denis lies immediately to the north and east of the city of Paris. At its capital, Saint-Denis, the magnificent twelfth-century abbey church (now cathedral) erected by Abbé Suger ushered in the age of gothic architecture, and is the resting place of the kings of France.

"This recipe, first of all, combines a ubiquitous ingredient, chicken, with one from afar, curry—so, like Seine-Saint-Denis, it has a mixture of origins! Second, curried chicken is even better when reheated, which makes it a great plate for a parliamentarian. Deputies don't have a dinner hour and often eat long after the family meal. At such times, the treat of a reheated chicken curry is at least a small consolation."

Patrice Calméjane
Deputy of Seine-Saint-Denis

Serves 8

2 onions, finely chopped
6 tablespoons butter
8 chicken thighs, skinned
Pepper and salt
3/4 cup dry white wine
1 teaspoon curry powder
2 tablespoons flour
6–8 cups chicken stock
1 cup crème fraiche
1 1/2 cups rice

✓ Preheat oven to 325°F.

✓ In a large skillet, melt 3 tablespoons butter and sauté 1 chopped onion until translucent. Add chicken pieces and cook, turning, until browned. Sprinkle with salt.

✓ Pour in wine and turn up heat to burn off alcohol. Sprinkle chicken with curry powder and flour. Slowly add 4 cups hot stock. Adjust seasoning. Simmer for 35 minutes.

✓ Meanwhile, make the rice. In an ovenproof casserole, sauté 1 chopped onion in 3 tablespoons butter. Add rice and stir to coat grains. Pour in a ladle of stock and let boil off for a few moments, then add 3 cups hot stock, cover, and bake in oven for about 20 minutes.

✓ When chicken is done, stir in crème fraiche if serving immediately. (If not, reheat later with more stock before stirring in cream.)

✓ Place a bed of rice on a serving plate, top with a chicken thigh, and coat with sauce. Serve.

Flan Flambé

Flaugnarde

Val-de-Marne, the department in the Île-de-France that directly abuts Paris on the southeast side, is where the river Marne finally joins forces with the Seine. Of particular interest to gastronomes, Val-de-Marne is home to the vast wholesale food markets at Rungis, which in 1969 replaced their storied central-Paris predecessor, Les Halles. The action is, of course, predawn.

"To make a good flaugnarde, you have to get up early . . . or so said my grandmother, who on autumn Sundays always used to prepare one for us kids. We would sit around her kitchen table and enjoy the flaugnarde—a sort of flan—while playing cards. Today I take pleasure in recreating the experience with my own family, using the same words she used to summon the tribe. Then I warm a small shot of rum, ignite it, and let the blue flames dance over the flaugnarde."

Marie-Anne Montchamp
Deputy of Val-de-Marne

✓ Preheat oven to 400°F.

✓ In a bowl, mix flour, salt, eggs, 1 tablespoon rum, 1 cup milk, and all but 2 tablespoons of the sugar. Stir well. When smooth, add remaining 1 cup milk.

✓ Butter a square cake tin and line with buttered parchment paper. Pour batter into cake tin. Dot with remaining butter.

✓ Place in oven, and lower temperature to 350°F. Bake flan about 30 minutes, testing with the point of a knife.

✓ Sprinkle reserved sugar over flan. In a small saucepan, heat 1 ounce rum for a few seconds. Turn heat off. Ignite rum and, while flaming, pour over flan.

Serves 6

1 1/2 cups flour
Pinch of salt
4 eggs
3 tablespoons rum
2 cups milk
3/4 cup sugar
3 tablespoons butter

Braised Duck with Cherries
Canard braisé aux montmorency

Val-d'Oise, directly north of Paris, is in the second tier of Île-de-France departments circling the city. Its rich land remains largely agricultural, but residential subdivision is on the rise. One victim is the town of Montmorency, just ten miles from Paris, where the cherries that bear its name are now grown in only a few orchards. Cultivation of the red sour Montmorency cherry is increasing elsewhere, however, as its high antioxidant level adds to its culinary appeal.

"This long-established preparation with sour cherries—emblematic of Montmorency—represents well our region. Cherries are particularly delicious with duck."

Jérôme Chartier
Deputy of Val-d'Oise

Serves 4

1 Muscovy duck, about 3 pounds
1 celery stalk
1 leek
3 carrots
3 turnips
1 onion
1 clove
2 juniper berries
1/4 teaspoon cinnamon
1 bouquet garni
5 cups red wine
2 cups chicken stock
Pepper and salt
6 tablespoons butter
2 pounds sour cherries, pitted
2 tablespoons sugar

✓ In a heavy casserole, put duck, vegetables, spices, and bouquet garni. Add wine and stock, pepper and salt. Bring to a boil, reduce to simmer, and cook 30 minutes.

✓ Preheat oven to 350°F.

✓ Remove duck from casserole. Carve into serving pieces. Place in an ovenproof dish and dot with half the butter.

✓ Roast for 1 hour, basting duck pieces with cooking juices every 10 minutes.

✓ In a skillet, melt remaining butter, add sugar and cherries, and sauté for 10 minutes. Lower heat to minimum and simmer another 10 minutes. Set aside and rewarm at serving time.

✓ Remove duck from oven and place on a serving platter. Pour cherries over and around duck. Serve.

Jellied Rabbit
Lapin en compote

"The region called the Vexin is an historical county in north-central France known for its ancient monuments—châteaux, churches, fortified farmsteads—but also rich in local production such as its excellent beer, its cider, and many preparations of rabbit. This typical Vexin jellied rabbit is offered at a specialty shop that sells its own farm-raised fowl and rabbit products, La Ferme du Lapin Compote, in a most charming Vexin village called Commeny."

Philippe Houillon
Deputy of Val-d'Oise

1 rabbit, about 3 pounds
1 tablespoon olive oil
1 tablespoon butter
1/4 pound bacon cubes (lardons)
5 shallots, peeled
3 carrots, peeled and sliced
1 1/4 cups dry white wine
1 sprig thyme
1 or 2 sprigs rosemary
6 bay leaves
2 garlic cloves, peeled
Pepper and salt
1 tablespoon gelatin

✓ Remove limbs from rabbit, cut off saddle section, then cut through breastbone and divide torso lengthwise.

✓ In a skillet, heat oil and butter. Sauté rabbit pieces, browning slightly on all sides. Add lardons, shallots, and carrots, and cook 5 more minutes. Add 1 cup wine, herbs, garlic, pepper, and salt. Simmer gently for 2 hours.

✓ Remove all bones from rabbit pieces, taking extra care with torso sections. Shred meat a little and distribute in terrine along with carrot slices, shallots, and lardons.

✓ Filter meat juices. In a small saucepan, dilute gelatin in 1/2 cup cold white wine and heat briefly. Add filtered meat juice. Pour liquid mixture over rabbit. Refrigerate overnight.

✓ Slice and serve with frites and a green salad.

Coconut Jam Cake
Tourment d'amour

Guadeloupe, a Caribbean island group in the Lesser Antilles, has been a French overseas department since 1946.
"This exquisite pastry, a specialty of the Îles des Saintes, is among the thousand and one jewels of Guadeloupe cuisine. The local ladies used to prepare it to tempt their men when they returned from their all-day fishing. No Guadeloupe palate was able to resist that pastry with its explosion of coconut, vanilla, and cinnamon in its hidden heart. Today, tourists too have discovered its special tenderness, and the Tourment d'Amour has become a favorite that can have at its sweet center any fruit flavor: guava, banana, pineapple—or passion fruit."

Gabrielle Louis-Carabin
Deputy of Guadeloupe

✓ In a saucepan, place all the ingredients for the coconut jam. Simmer 30 minutes, stirring so it doesn't burn. When it is thick but not too dry, set aside to cool.
✓ Preheat oven to 325°F.
✓ Line a tart mold with pâte brisée or one-pie dough, crimping to make an attractive border. Spread bottom evenly with coconut jam.
✓ Prepare the crunchy topping. In a mixing bowl, whisk eggs, sugar, and vanilla until pale and foamy. Sprinkle flour in and mix well. Spread this batter over coconut jam layer.
✓ Bake 30–40 minutes. Cool. Unmold and sprinkle with some coconut.

"You can succumb to this Torment of Love along with a cup of hot chocolate or a light rum punch."

Serves 6
1/2 pound pastry dough for a one-crust pie
5 eggs
3/4 cup sugar
1 teaspoon vanilla extract
1 1/4 cups flour
Grated coconut for garnish
For the coconut jam:
3 cups shredded coconut, unsweetened
1 1/4 cups sugar
1 cup water
1/4 cup rum
1/4 teaspoon cinnamon
1 vanilla bean, split lengthwise
Zest of 1 lemon

Pâté of Lamb and Innards in a Casserole

Pâté en pot, ou patte en pot

The French department of Martinique, a volcanic island of some 430 square miles in the Lesser Antilles, is a little bit of France with a Caribbean flair. The pâté en pot, *not for the faint-hearted, because it consists of meat and innards, is a delicious dish that is invariably served on festive occasions. "Truly emblematic of our island, this recipe can be found nowhere else."*

Alfred Almont
Deputy of Martinique

✓ Wash all lamb parts under running water for 10 minutes. Let soak in a container of water with the lemon juice overnight. Rinse again. Reserve liver.
✓ In a kettle, place lamb parts, 1 onion studded with cloves, carrots, bouquet garni, pepper, and salt. Add water to cover and cook 2 hours (or, in a pressure cooker, 40 minutes).
✓ Chop scallions and remaining onion. In a heavy-bottomed pot, sauté in oil until translucent.
✓ Peel and cube the turnips, leeks, cabbage, malanga, and giraumon. Add to the pot and cook 5 minutes. Add wine and bois d'Inde leaves, then moisten with half lamb stock, half water.
✓ Lift lamb parts from stock. Remove all bones and cut meats into small pieces. Add to vegetables, along with diced ham and bacon. Blanch liver, cut into small pieces, and add it too. Pour in rest of lamb stock and cook for 20 minutes. Add potatoes. After 10 minutes, add garlic and hot pepper, and simmer 1 hour more.
✓ As you are about to serve, add capers.

Note: Malanga (Sp. *yautía*), a tuber, is found in Caribbean or Hispanic groceries and some general markets; yam is the closest equivalent. Giraumon is a kind of pumpkin; any cooking pumpkin (Sp. *calabaza*) will do. The bush misleadingly called "bois d'Inde" is native to the Antilles, where its leaves (and its berries, called Jamaica pepper) are much used. The leaves' flavor is described as a mixture of anise, clove, and lemongrass, so if they cannot be found, use lemongrass.

Serves 8
1 lamb's head (without brain)
4 lamb's feet
Lamb tripe, stomach, and liver
Juice of 2 lemons
3 carrots
2 onions
6 cloves
1 large bouquet garni (parsley, celery, thyme, bay leaves)
Pepper and salt
3 scallions
1/4 cup olive oil
2 turnips
2 leeks, whites only, well washed
4 cabbage leaves
1 malanga (see note)
1 pound giraumon (see note)
1/2 cup white wine
2 leaves bois d'Inde (see note)
1 pound ham, diced
1/3 pound slab bacon, diced
3 potatoes, diced
3 garlic cloves, minced
1 hot red pepper
2 tablespoons capers

Curried Pork with Vegetables

Colombo de porc

*French Guiana is an overseas department of France located on the northern
Atlantic coast of South America, bordered on the west by Suriname and on the
south and east by Brazil.*

*In the eighteenth century the French under Napoleon III turned a good part of
French Guiana into penal colonies, including Devil's Island, ten miles offshore. Of
the 80,000 mostly political prisoners who went through its system, fewer than
10 percent survived their sentences. The horror of that penal settlement became
famous when the French unjustly sent Captain Alfred Dreyfus there, for treason.
The prison was closed in 1952.*

*Since 1968 the coast is more positively known for the state-of-the-art space base
at Kourou, the launch site for the European Space Agency.*

*"For those who lovingly evoke Guyanaise cuisine, it is the traditional broth
specially prepared for Pentecost or big celebrations, made with awara—the fruit
of a specific Amazon palm tree indigenous to Guyane— that comes to mind. It
takes two days and nights to prepare awara soup with all its vegetables, three fish,
different meats. I invite everyone to come to Guyane to taste it.*

*"Meanwhile, I offer our colombo, a dish that reflects the East Indian influence in
our creole culture."*

Christiane Taubira
Deputy of Guyane

Serves 4

1 pound pork roast
Juice of 2 lemons
2 garlic cloves
2 tablespoons curry powder
1 teaspoon cayenne pepper
Pepper and salt
1/3 cup olive oil
1 pound potatoes
2 onions
3 cucumbers
1 eggplant
1 green mango
5 scallions
1 cup parsley, finely chopped

✓ In a bowl, marinate pork overnight with juice of 1 lemon, 1 clove garlic, 1 tablespoon curry powder, cayenne, and pepper and salt.

✓ In a skillet, heat oil. Lightly brown meat on all sides, 15 minutes. Add potatoes and onions, and sauté for 10 minutes. Add eggplant, cucumbers, and mango. Dilute the remaining 1 teaspoon curry powder in 1/2 cup hot water and stir in gently. Add enough water to cover pork. Cover. Simmer 35 minutes. Toward the end, add the remaining garlic clove, crushed, along with the scallions and parsley. When the heat is turned off, add the remaining lemon juice, and pepper and salt to taste.

✓ Serve the pork colombo with jasmine rice—and, for those who wish, with chopped raw chiles.

Spicy Casserole of Cod with Garlic and Tomato
Rougail de morue

In the seventeenth century the king of France, Louis XIII, named this mountainous island of volcanic origin Île Bourbon. In 1793 it was renamed Île de la Réunion. A French department, Réunion is in the Indian Ocean, east of Madagascar.

Rougail, a spicy tomato preparation, is a traditional Réunion treatment of salted and dried cod, called morue *in French and* bacalao *or variants in other Mediterranean languages. This recipe was provided by Didier Robert, deputy of Réunion.*

Serves 4

1 pound salt cod
6 onions, minced
3 tablespoon olive oil
5 garlic cloves, crushed
1 sprig thyme
6 tomatoes, cut into quarters
7 hot red peppers, seeded and cut into strips
1 cup water

✓ Immerse dried cod in a bowl of water for 24 hours to remove salt, changing water from time to time.

✓ In a kettle, cook cod in simmering water for 20 minutes. Drain. Remove skin and bones, and crumble fish into flakes.

✓ In a skillet, heat the oil. Sauté onions until translucent. Add cod. Add garlic and thyme, then tomatoes, stirring over fairly high heat, then finally hot peppers and water. Stir frequently and watch that it doesn't burn. The dish is ready to serve when all water has evaporated.

Twice-Cooked Sausage with Tomato in a Spicy Sauce

Rougail saucisses

"In some parts of our island, saffron, ginger, and garlic often appear in various dishes. Be sure to incorporate saffron before the tomatoes. Ginger, finely sliced, will go into the preparation at the same time as the hot pepper."

René-Paul Victoria
Deputy of Réunion

Serves 4

6 sausages, either fresh or smoked kielbasa
3 tablespoons olive oil
3 onions, sliced
1 hot pepper, seeded and chopped
Salt
1 pound tomatoes, diced

✓ Blanch the sausages for 5 minutes. If they are quite salty, repeat, pricking them with a fork. Rinse. Put the sausages back to cook in a little water for 10 minutes until the water boils off. In a skillet, heat the oil and sauté the sausages. Add the onions, and the hot pepper mashed with salt. When the onions are golden brown, add the tomato. Cook uncovered over low heat for another 20 minutes, or until the sauce has thickened nicely. Serve.

Gratin of Halibut and Potato
Rôti de flétan

Situated in the northwestern Atlantic Ocean, just south of Newfoundland, Saint-Pierre-et-Miquelon is the only remnant of the former French colonial empire in North America. As an overseas territorial collectivity, it is self-governing under French control. Flétan, which strictly means halibut, is their name for any kind of flatfish found there. Rôti, or roast, means the whole fish, all but the head section rolled and presented like a meat roast. If halibut is not available, cod may be substituted, or whole monkfish tail, or two whole filets of halibut placed together to approximate the rôti.
"One of my childhood memories, the roast of flétan was usually prepared by my mother on Wednesdays or Fridays—considered fish days. I recall the great activity in our harbor, crowded with Portuguese, Spanish, Japanese, Korean, German, Russian trawlers as they offloaded their catch and reprovisioned. This was a time when fishing in the North Atlantic was still an important source of economic affluence for us."

Annick Girardin
Deputy of Saint-Pierre-et-Miquelon

✓ Preheat oven to 350°F.
✓ In a kettle of salted water, cook potatoes in their skins for 15 minutes. Drain. Peel and slice.
✓ In a skillet, heat 3 tablespoons butter. Sauté onions until translucent.
✓ Rub an ovenproof dish with the garlic. Line the dish with potato slices. Place fish on top, then add onions.
✓ In a bowl, combine milk and crème fraiche, a little salt and pepper. Pour over fish. Dot with bits of butter. Roast for about 30 minutes. Serve sprinkled with parsley.

Serves 6
6 potatoes
4 onions, sliced
4 tablespoons butter
1 clove garlic
1 whole halibut, beheaded and gutted, or 2 pounds cod
2 cups milk
1/2 cup crème fraiche
Salt
Pepper
1 cup parsley, finely chopped

Casserole of Mackerel, Coconut Milk, Mango, and Tapioca

Mataba au poisson

Mayotte, a small island group in the Indian Ocean, is a French overseas department. Part of the Comoros Islands in the Mozambique Channel between Madagascar and the African mainland, Mayotte chose to remain part of France when the rest of the Comoros became independent in 1975. "Matabu is no doubt the favorite dish on our island. We serve it often, and especially on occasions like weddings, anniversaries, and other celebrations."

Abdoulatifou Aly
Deputy of Mayotte

Serves 4

1 mackerel, about 3 pounds (if possible, ask your fishmonger to remove the bones, otherwise, it is up to you to remove at home).
4 cups unsweetened coconut milk
2 garlic cloves, smashed
1 large onion, finely chopped
Salt
½ cup of pounded manioc leaves

✓ In a kettle of salted water, cook fish 10 minutes. Drain. Pull the meat off the bones and crumble it, feeling carefully with the fingertips to be sure all the tiny fishbones are removed. Reserve.

✓ In a large, heavy-bottomed saucepan, heat coconut milk, garlic, onion, and salt to taste. Bring to a boil, reduce heat, and stir in manioc. Cook for 1 hour, stirring occasionally. Incorporate crumbled fish, stir well, and let liquid reduce over low heat until dry. Turn heat off.

✓ Serve over rice, with pickled mangoes or lemons.

Tip: If you can find *brède mafane*—a strong and rather peppery herb available in Asian markets, known also as Spilanthes or as Pará cress from its use in Brazilian cuisine—crumble a few leaves and add them to the coconut milk along with the fish.

Breadfruit in Coconut Milk

Sausau

A French overseas territory, the Wallis and Futuna Islands in the South Pacific are situated to the northeast of New Caledonia, to which they were administratively attached until 1961.
Breadfruit grows on the breadfruit tree, an evergreen of the mulberry family that is found throughout the South Pacific, in Southeast Asia. The breadfruit has to be peeled. What is edible is the gelatinous meat inside, which when scooped out of the breadfruit can be grilled or boiled, and can be enjoyed either salted or sweetened with some natural syrup. This recipe was provided by Apeleto Albert Likuvalu, deputy of Wallis-et-Futuna.

✓ Put breadfruit on the grill for 10 minutes on each side. Peel. With a stick, tap to soften. Open, and cut into cubes. In a saucepan, cook breadfruit cubes with coconut milk for 1 hour. Cool for 10 minutes. Serve.

Serves 10
3 breadfruits
Milk of 2 coconuts

Ceviche of White Fish Cubes in Coconut Milk

Poisson cru au lait de coco

French Polynesia, an overseas territory in the middle of the South Pacific, straddles the Tropic of Capricorn and, in its vast sweep from the Austral Islands to the Marquesas, encompasses the Society Islands, of which the most celebrated is Tahiti.

"Typically Polynesian, this recipe can be enjoyed at different meals. It can also be adapted with other local products. I recommend the version with langoustines (crawfish) and lemon juice. But shrimp or lobster meat is delicious as well."

Michel Buillard
Deputy of Polynésie

✓ In a bowl, combine fish cubes with juice of 5 limes and 3/4 cup coconut milk. Refrigerate until well marinated, about 40 minutes. Drain fish.

✓ Place fish in center of serving platter. Arrange vegetables around fish. Mix juice of 1 lime with remaining 1/4 cup coconut milk, season with pepper and salt to taste, and sprinkle over the vegetables. Serve.

Variation: You can place lettuce leaves on platter with fish, and dress with a classic vinaigrette.

Serves 6
1 1/2 pounds tuna or other firm fish, without skin or bones, cut into cubes
Juice of 6 limes
1 cup unsweetened coconut milk
1 onion, finely sliced
3 carrots, peeled and cut into thin sticks
1 cucumber, peeled and cut into thin sticks
1 tomato, peeled and cubed
1/2 red bell pepper, seeded and cut into sticks
Pepper and salt

Ceviche of Tuna Slices with Lemongrass

Filet de thon mariné à la citronelle

New Caledonia, a French overseas territory, is a collectivity of islands located in the extreme western part of the South Pacific. It is directly east of Australia across the Coral Sea. Its population is a blend of Melanesian and European—as is its cuisine.

Fish holds a big presence in all those islands cuisine. The abundance of spices often offers similarity in flavor. This recipe was provided by Gaël Yanno, deputy of Nouvelle-Calédonie.

✓ With a sharp knife, slice tuna very thinly. On serving plates, fan out the fish slices. You should have 4 slices per person.

✓ In a bowl, whisk lime and lemon juice, olive oil, fennel seeds, lemongrass, pepper, and salt into a marinade. Pour marinade over each slice of fish.

✓ Snip the green parts of the scallions into thin rings. Leave the white parts whole, but make two longitudinal slits almost to the root end, then immerse them in iced water so that they open like flowers.

✓ Place scallion fans decoratively over fish. Add tomato cubes and cherry tomatoes. Sprinkle with parsley and scallion rings.

✓ Serve well chilled.

Serves 6

2–3 pounds tuna
Juice of 7 limes
Juice of 1 lemon
1/2 cup olive oil
1/4 cup fennel seeds
2 stalks lemongrass, peeled and finely sliced
Pepper and salt

For the garnish:
2 tomatoes, peeled, seeded, and diced
6 cherry tomatoes
1/2 cup finely chopped parsley
6 scallions

THANKS

I wish to thank Bernard Accoyer, president of the National Assembly; all of the deputies from every political party who participated in the making of this book; my friend Bernard Debré, deputy of Paris, for his encouragement; and Julie Torossian, Solveig de Drouas, Annie Moret, and Christophe Delclève, my devoted collaborators.

INDEX